"This W H Smith/Doubleday Book Club
Edition   it

GW01465216

CORE BUSINESS STUDIES

MARKETING

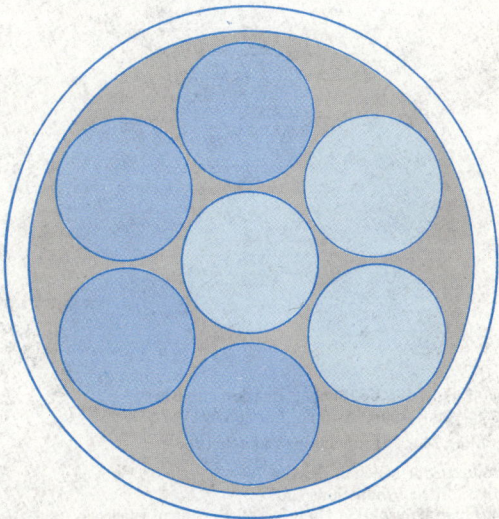

E. T. Martin O.ST.J., MSc, DMS, MBIM

Mitchell Beazley

The producers of Core Business Studies
wish to thank those members of the
British Institute of Management who have
given their advice and their time to ensure
that each book in the series meets the high
standards required by modern British
business.

Published 1983 by Mitchell Beazley Publishers
87-89 Shaftesbury Avenue, London W1V 7AD
© Mike Morris Productions Limited 1983

Produced for Mitchell Beazley by
Mike Morris Productions Ltd.
Burnham House, 93a High Street, Burnham, Bucks.

All rights reserved
No part of this work may be reproduced
or utilized in any form by any means,
electronic or mechanical, including
photocopying, recording or by any
information storage and retrieval system,
without the prior written permission of
the publisher.

ISBN 0 85533 442 8

Designed by Stewart Cowley & Associates
Typeset by Barnes Design + Print Group
Printed and bound in Great Britain.

Contents

Introduction

Whether we are considering Ford Motor Co. or ICI, the local football team or a dental practice, a fundamental process which is common to all of them is that of **marketing**. Each has goods (or services) which it is prepared to offer to potential and existing customers, because the 'organization' recognizes that customers have **needs and/or wants** which require to be satisfied. However, marketing is not simply 'selling': that is one small (but important) part of the whole marketing process. What then is marketing?

Marketing is that part of the managerial process which attempts to *identify, anticipate and supply* the consumer's requirements, efficiently and profitably. (Institute of Marketing)

It has also been described as:

. . .the performance of business activities which direct the flow of goods or services from the producer to the consumer.

Business organizations need to recognize that the only constant thing in life is change. Public tastes and technology necessitate a constant re-appraisal of a product's utility. Competitiveness, particularly from overseas and the EEC, has become a significant factor in influencing **corporate goals**, both long- and short-term, and plans and control procedures necessary to achieve such targets. Today's businesses exist in a dynamic and evolving society and the marketing function in any enterprise must recognize the uncertain nature of such a society. No marketing policy can, therefore, remain fixed for long, for marketing is (or should be) *in the vanguard* of the firm's activities, acting as the antennae of the organism, regulating its internal workings and influencing its relationships with other organizations and individuals in the society in which it operates.

The aim of this book is to act primarily as a revision aid for those studying for business and management examinations; as an aid, its text is telegrammatic and precise. Readers are urged to use the **Further Reading** section on page 119 for a more detailed and discursive account of the various and varied concepts and methods. Because of its concise form, it is hoped that the book will also appeal to the interested layman, whether he is a businessman or not, who wishes simply to understand the fundamentals of marketing without the need to examine the subject in great depth and whose time and commitment may well be limited.

I am grateful to my students without whose stimulation (and provocation) the book would not have been written and to Jim O'Kane whose encouragement made it possible.

Chapter 1

The Systems Approach

Of all the functional areas of a firm, marketing is the most **pervasive** and **dynamic** activity. It is a well-known concept that marketing leads all other functions of a commercial organization in terms of time but not, of course, in terms of importance. It is on the **information** culled and the analysis undertaken by the marketing department that the company's resources, and their acquisition and allocation to the various departments – such as production, personnel, research and development and finance – must be made.

The corporate departments or divisions may be considered as **sub-systems** which collectively comprise the total system of the organization, rather like the various systems of the body or a motor car. The essence of the management task is to control, co-ordinate, monitor and ensure that all the sub-systems contribute **meaningfully** to the total output of the enterprise and to the attainment of the **corporate objectives**, whatever they might be. It may well be that the members of some departments may agree with neither the organizational, tactical objectives nor with those operational objectives of the formal group to which they have been allocated, but in establishing the firm's goals the top management must take into consideration the diverse expectations of the stakeholders, i.e. the shareholders, employees, customers, etc. and, to some extent, diverging group and individual aims must be expected. The **conflict** which may result must not be regarded as unhealthy, for **controlled**, manifest conflict is often *catalytic* in its effects. It is *latent* and inhibited conflict which may precipitate low morale, poor output and individual disaffection with the enterprise.

The departments, or sub-systems, must interconnect like cogwheels in an engine. It is of little use, and indeed may be positively detrimental, if one cogwheel spins incessantly yet fails to contribute to the total effort required to turn the main shaft of the engine, which in turn pushes the firm forward. An organization is never static or stagnant: it will tend to go either forward or backward. It is the responsibility of marketing to ensure that the firm always advances and never retreats, even for a tactical re-grouping. An enterprise will tend to reach its peak of fitness if the sub-systems are able to receive and digest adequate and reliable information and to respond appropriately, in much the same way that a living organism must, if it is to develop, reproduce, regenerate and indeed survive.

The systems approach to the study of organizations was hinted at by Barnard in 1938, Simon in the 1950s and Dahrendorf in 1958, but the concept of systems as **socio-technical amalgams** has been developed by members of the Tavistock Institute of Human Relations (Trist and Bamforth) and originated from their work in the coal-mining industry when they investigated the long-wall method of mining coal. They found that three separate shift-working groups were responsible for cutting the coal, filling the hoppers and conveyor-moving of the coal but never all three tasks in the same work-cycle. Although the groups relied upon each other, each shift was structured as a discrete unit with its own bonuses and payment system, and this tended to produce not only rivalry but also intergroup hostility which clearly affected productivity. The groups were reorganized to form one composite group, all the members of which could do all the tasks required. The new social structure allowed for the optimum use of the machinery, i.e. the technical aspects of the job.

The enterprise is a **system**. A system consists of a set of **interdependent parts** which have **needs** and which will exhibit **behaviour patterns** in order to fulfil those needs. Etzioni (1964) states that the organization must concentrate upon its **needs**, rather than its **goals**. The system needs stability, otherwise it becomes off-balance (consider the intricate and interdependent relationships of the sub-systems of the human body).

No sub-system can (or should) operate independently of other sub-systems: it should not exist in isolation. Neither should business enterprises, which are essentially **open** systems that must interact with their **environment**, for they must receive information and, as part of the firm's **communications mix**, must disseminate information about their products, pricing, labour relations and social awareness. It is the successful integration of the various and varied sub-systems – marketing, production, finance research, personnel, etc. – which will do much to ensure the overall success of the firm (however that success might be measured). The integration of the departments invariably demands that the **marketing function spearheads** the firm's activities, but this concept requires that every member of the organization sees the enterprise as a whole and understands how the various functions of the company and its marketing organization depend upon one another (Figure 1).

However, every department is dependent on the organization having clear, unambiguous and preferably quantifiable objectives. This necessitates some long-range planning, even in the turbulent and uncertain economic climate of today. Short-term opportunism will lead simply to management by crisis and exception. Goal-setting, and the associated planning, requires careful and detailed analysis of all relevant information if the firm's decision-making is to be rational and profitable (or less costly).

THE DECISION-MAKING PROCESS

It is the people in the organization who are responsible for making and implementing decisions based upon the information received and their perception and analysis of

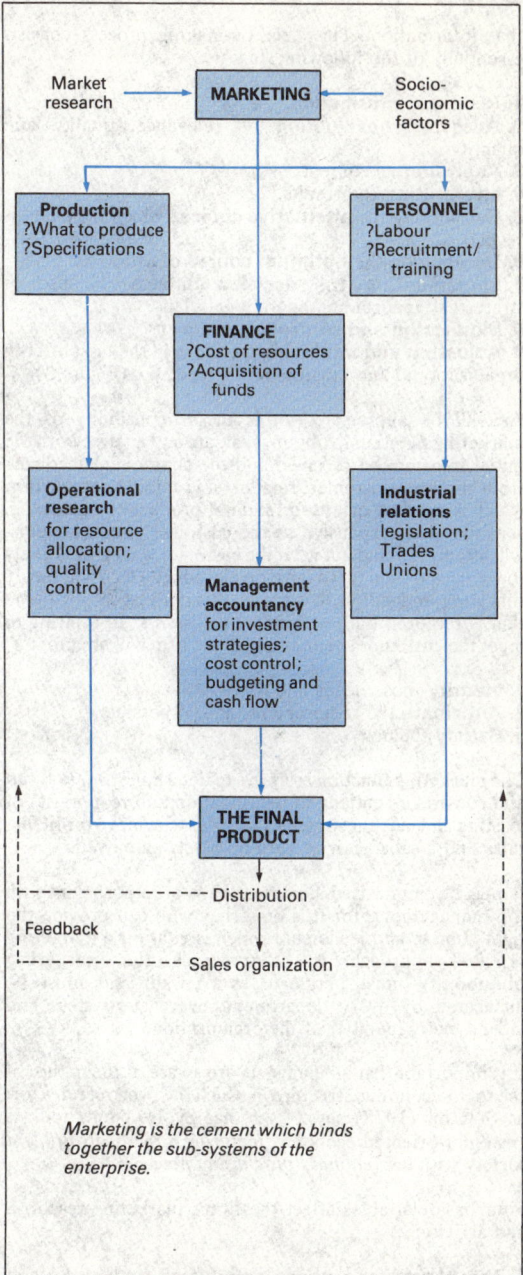

Market research → **MARKETING** ← Socio-economic factors

Production
?What to produce
?Specifications

PERSONNEL
?Labour
?Recruitment/
training

FINANCE
?Cost of resources
?Acquisition of funds

Operational research
for resource allocation; quality control

Industrial relations
legislation;
Trades Unions

Management accountancy
for investment strategies;
cost control;
budgeting and cash flow

THE FINAL PRODUCT

Distribution

Feedback

Sales organization

Marketing is the cement which binds together the sub-systems of the enterprise.

Figure 1. The systems approach

that information. This decision-making process consists essentially of the following stages:

1. Receiving **information**.
2. Adequately **evaluating** its relevance, quality and quantity.
3. Analysing its content.
4. Interpreting the results.
5. Considering the **alternative choices** which the analysis reveals.
6. Deciding on the **optimum course** of action.
7. Implementing the decision through the use of strategical, tactical and operational plans.
8. Monitoring and controlling the plans.
9. Adjusting and modifying the plans in the light of both organizational and environmental feedback (Figure 3).

As will be appreciated, it is the responsibility of the marketing function to obtain, evaluate and analyse both the initial information received and the subsequent feedback from the final customer, retailers and middlemen. A firm which is **market-oriented** (and not product-oriented), i.e. sensitive and responsive to the customer's requirements, will attempt to find out what the customer wants (or is likely to want) and then try to develop a product which will satisfy that want and still yield a profit. It is not just sales volume that is required but *profitable sales volume*. In aspiring to meet the customer's requirements the firm will attempt to:

1. Identify those needs and wants.
2. Anticipate the requirements and, if possible,
3. Satisfy them.

The marketing function is always to determine a *market gap* and consists essentially of investigation and reappraisal of existing and current strategies in order to achieve profitable sales and a satisfactory return on assets employed.

It must be emphasized, however, that marketing begins with top management, for it is only they who can provide the right climate and leadership which is vital for a marketing oriented approach. In other words, the **marketing philosophy** must permeate every wall, and must be inculcated by every department, every sub-system and indeed every member of the organization.

It is important that all managers are aware of the nature of the socio-economic structure in which the firm operates for, as Stanton (1978) says, '. . .it has evolved into today's customer-oriented economy, featuring a relatively *affluent* society with *discretionary purchasing power*. . .'.

Four basic variables affect the firm's marketing response and activity:

1. The consumer's needs and wants—influenced and stimulated by his *values, beliefs, attitudes* and *perception*.

2. The general economic situation, in particular *government policy* and the various measures it takes in order to attain its primary objectives of:

(a) *stable prices;* controlling inflation,
(b) *economic growth,*
(c) *balance of payments* equilibrium,
(d) *full employment.*

3. Competition – both at home and from overseas.

4. The rate and nature of technological change and the need to update its product and/or production/marketing methods.

In a highly competitive and consumer-oriented society there is always an ongoing need for the enterprise to study and develop potential markets, the development of which is influenced significantly by the micro and macroeconomic changes which occur. Changes of recent note include:

1. Environmental (i.e. external)

(a) Decreasing employment opportunities resulting in limited increase in discretionary spending power and aggregate demand.
(b) Attempts to maximize the use of increasingly scarce resources, e.g. energy, raw materials.
(c) Incredible technological developments, e.g. petrochemicals, the microchip and electronic engineering.
(d) The growth of international competition (particularly from Third World countries).
(e) Increased export opportunities, e.g. the EEC.
(f) Pernicious inflation associated with increasing credit expansion, interest rates and international events.

2. Organizational (i.e. internal)

(a) Tendency for firms to be bigger and more complex; greater specialization and division of labour; increased automation; increased redundancy of manpower.
(b) The growth of multi-nationals and their ability to control and manipulate vast resources which may have a marked affect on the economy of one or more countries.
(c) The impact and influence of trades unions; the move towards greater worker participation and industrial legislation.
(d) Growing awareness of the need for management training.
(e) Increasing need to be more flexible and competitive, and to achieve a diminution of bureaucratic procedures in order to increase the firm's adaptability.

Market orientation requires careful and detailed attention to the marketing effort, making sure that most of it is directed to the potentially profitable activities so that the returns achieved are proportional to and reflect the marketing effort involved. Such a philosophy requires the judicious use of market and marketing research.

THE MARKETING MIX

To this end the marketing mix requires detailed analysis and projection before it can be finally agreed. This mix consists of four key variables:

1. **The product.**
2. **Its price.**
3. **Its promotion.**   **The marketing mix**
4. **The place.**

Another variable, **packaging**, is sometimes added but it belongs essentially to the promotional aspects as part of the communications mix. It is through the correct permutation and interaction of the individual mix elements that marketing fulfils its role of profitably finding, creating and keeping customers. These mix elements can only be selected, however, in the light of the company's possession or acquisition of adequate and suitable resources. What must also be appreciated is that mix elements are interdependent: alter one and another (or more) is changed.

The marketing policy in a consumer-oriented company has been defined as:

1. Determining the kinds of *product* which
the firm should attempt to sell.   **WHAT?**
2. Defining the *customers* at whom the
marketing effort should be directed.   **TO WHOM?**
3. Defining the *action and procedures* to
be implemented in order to get the
products to the customer.   **HOW?**

In essence, it is the *future* which determines what the firm should be doing *now*. The firm, therefore, must study both existing and potential markets at home and abroad in order to identify, create and retain customers. In addition, the firm must frequently ask what business it is really in. For example, is British Rail simply involved in railroads or is it also concerned, say, with transportation and materials handling systems? Is British Telecom simply selling telephone systems, or sophisticated communication networks as well? The firm must always attempt to maximize its use of available resources and seek market opportunities which may not be readily apparent. It must determine which sections of the market it is best equipped to serve and what resources, in terms of manpower, machinery, plant, finance, etc. it will require in order to penetrate and capture potential markets. The dynamic nature of the marketing function becomes increasingly apparent as the marketing management, in particular, attempts to respond to changes in the environment, to forecast the nature and longevity of these changes and to adjust and modify the internal structure and marketing organization of the firm so that it is capable of responding to these environmental changes.

The demands upon a marketing manager are significant, for he must not only be a specialist in his own field but possess considerable knowledge of other disciplines which impinge upon his own. According to Giles (1974), the marketing function must be aware (or capable) of:

1. The numerate implications and the manipulation of mathematical and statistical data, the use of **operational research** in order to maximize the use of scarce resources (or minimize associated costs) and the use and interpretation of **management accountancy** data, e.g. budgets, forecasting, ratio analysis, etc.

2. The relevance and interpretation of theories of **psychology** and **sociology**, particularly the effects on consumer behaviour, such as the values, beliefs, attitudes and other culturally determined influences which are idiosyncratic to a community or sub-group.

3. The effects of government **legislation** and international events which may have significance for the **macro-economic** situation and directly or indirectly affect the firm's ability to compete and the consumer's propensity to purchase, e.g. central government fiscal and monetary policy, i.e. interest rates and credit restrictions; the effects of inflation and associated counter-measures; the effects on demand and the relationships between supply, demand and pricing (Figure 1).

Essentially, the marketing function may be crystallized using an adapted mnemonic (source unknown):

P.O.I.S.E.

P—Philosophy One that is *customer/market oriented;* that attempts to identify and anticipate the customer's requirements; that permeates the enterprise from the chairman to the shop-floor operative.

O—Organization Is there a marketing organization which has clear and defined roles within the total system? Is it cost effective and how are such costs measured? Is it dynamic and does it contribute to the attainment of the corporate objectives?

I—Information Is the marketing and market information *up-to-date, adequate* and *relevant*? Is there any system of information retrieval and, if so, how effective and efficient is it?

S—Strategy Is there an efficient and effective strategy to capture, dominate and retain the market? Is the marketing objective quantified? What pricing strategies are adopted and with what goals in mind?

E—Efficiency in terms of sales and advertising effectiveness. Does it maximize the return on the resource inputs? What is the primary purpose of the advertising campaign and are the promotional and production aspects of the firm closely co-ordinated?

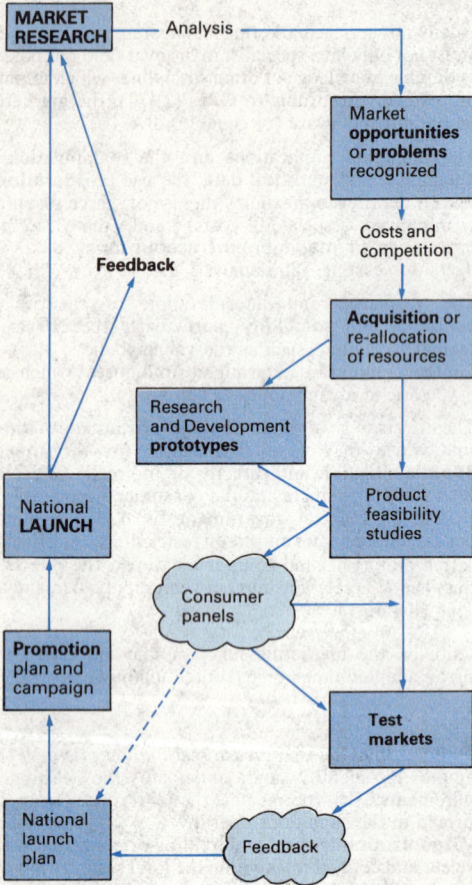

The marketing process is a dynamic
and sequential series of events.
The key element, which may influence
any event, is **INFORMATION** and its
subsequent treatment.

Figure 2. The marketing theme in practice

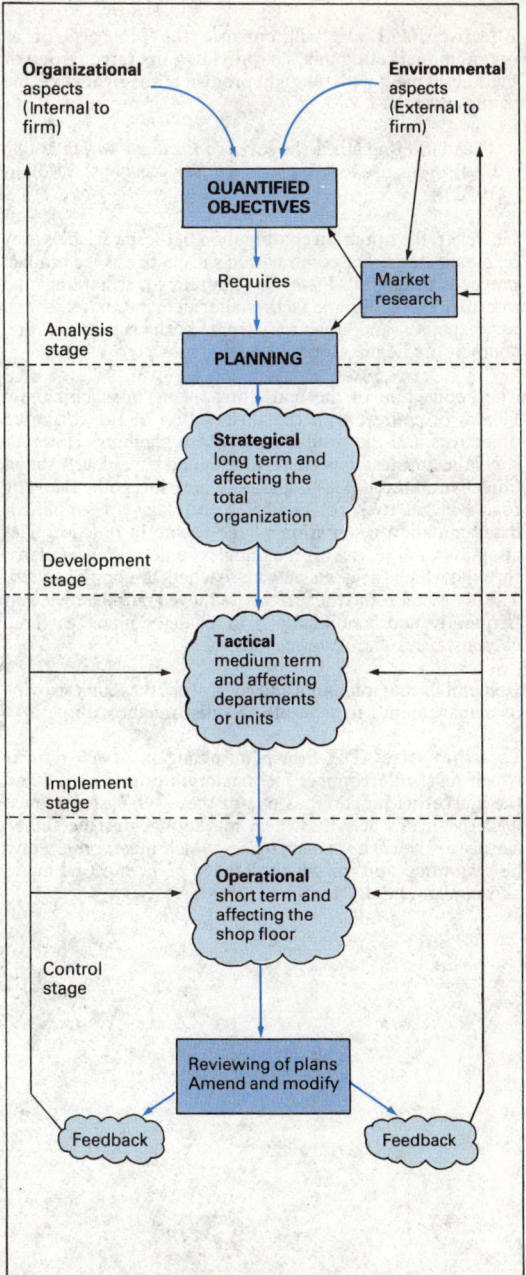

Organizational aspects (Internal to firm)

Environmental aspects (External to firm)

QUANTIFIED OBJECTIVES

Requires

Market research

Analysis stage

PLANNING

Strategical long term and affecting the total organization

Development stage

Tactical medium term and affecting departments or units

Implement stage

Operational short term and affecting the shop floor

Control stage

Reviewing of plans Amend and modify

Feedback

Feedback

Figure 3. Corporate planning and control

Effective P.O.I.S.E. will enhance the prospects of an optimum marketing mix, i.e. providing the target group or market segment with the right product at the right price and at the right time.

The marketing mix is the set of *controllable variables* that the firm can use to *influence the buyer's* response. (Kotler, 1972)

However, the optimum combination of these variables is by no means static. The combination will change as the product proceeds through its *life-cycle* (Chapter 6), as national and international economic factors alter demand patterns, and as response and reaction from both customers and competitors begins to take effect.

The application of the marketing theme must be closely linked, of course, with the formulation of the corporate objectives and the resulting corporate planning. However small the business, it is vital that it should have clearly stated objectives, for if it does not know where it is going then any road will get it there! Figures 2 and 3 give a simplified, diagrammatic presentation of the theme in practice. The adoption of objectives is meaningless unless *relevant* plans, through which the goals may be reached, are implemented. The plans made and the progress achieved must be reviewed frequently and modifications or changes made as time, circumstances and resources allow.

Remember that 'planning and control are the Siamese twins of management': to separate them is fraught with peril.

To summarize: The firm is an amalgam of *sub-systems* which must interconnect for maximum effectiveness, and the marketing function, as one of these sub-systems, must lead the firm's activities. The marketing must be linked closely to the *corporate objectives* which must, preferably, be quantified and for which detailed *plans* must be made and implemented.

Chapter 2

Market Research

The search for information

'When your marketing problems are known, they are half-solved!'

An individual cannot take correct action, except by chance, without receiving adequate and relevant **information** through his five basic senses. But to receive the information is simply not enough; the information must be processed, in other words, **evaluated** and **analysed**, and the **options** revealed. Only then should a course of action be selected. To operate in an information vacuum is potentially suicidal, not only for an individual but also for a commercial organization. 'To manage a business well is to manage its future, and to manage the future is to manage information' (Harper, 1961).

A company must develop and maintain a continuous **marketing information system** in order to generate and process information which will aid management decision-making, particularly in the field of marketing.

A survey in 1973 of 1322 American companies showed that in their marketing research:

    68% measured market potential.
    67% analysed market share.
    56% used it for pricing studies.
    49% measured the effectiveness of advertising
    (Twedt, 1973).

Not only can market research reduce the number of choices available and increase sales, it may also reveal wastage in certain areas – wastage which will reduce profit margins by increasing costs in marketing, production or other functional areas.

Crisp has defined market research as, '. . .the systematic, objective and exhaustive search for and study of the facts relevant to any problem in the field of marketing'.

Marketing research may provide information in the following major areas:

1. Product studies as regards developing and testing new products, and measuring consumer preference for both the product and the packaging.

2. Market analysis, in an attempt to measure current and potential sales, and to identify the appropriate market segment, i.e. the consumer, his characteristics and the target areas.

3. Advertising studies, to measure the effectiveness of the choice of media, the advertising campaign and the audience characteristics.

Collection of data

The input of relevant data is not an intermittent or periodic event; it occurs all the time and the data are readily available from such sources as the media and news reports. Data are usually available from many other sources and, depending upon their source and method of collection, can be classified as **primary** or **secondary** data.

Primary data are original data gathered specifically for current investigation. Secondary data are those already gathered by someone else and which are invariably cheaper to obtain than primary data. Secondary data, as well as being obtainable from many sources such as the Central Office of Information, government publications, trade journals (e.g. *The Grocer, Management Today*), public libraries and television companies, are also readily available from within the firm, using information stored on sales records from the customer relations department. **Methods of collecting primary data** are given below.

SURVEYS

A survey consists of obtaining information by interviewing a number of people (a **sample** of the particular population under investigation). Surveys are usually expensive and time-consuming and should not be undertaken lightly. In addition, the probability of error may be significant and **questionnaires** must be formulated with care in order to avoid **bias** and unsolicited or inadequate answers.

There are four main methods of gathering information:

1. By **personal interviews**.
2. By **post**.
3. By **telephone**.
4. **Panel data**.

1. Personal interviews These allow an **experienced** interviewer to modify the questions according to interviewee response, enabling a more in-depth gathering of information. However, if the interviewer strays from the carefully balanced questions, then elements of bias from either respondent or interviewer may creep in. This method is usually both very expensive and comparatively slow.

2. Postal surveys While this particular method tends to be slow in revealing results, postal surveys remain the cheapest form of investigation. Unfortunately, the response rate is usually very low and this may invalidate, or bring into question, the significance of the subsequent analysis. However, providing that the questionnaires are framed correctly, interviewer bias may be discounted. It is sometimes easier to reach certain groups of people with this method, providing an up-to-date mailing list is available.

3. Telephone surveys Clearly, a **random** sample of the total population is not possible because not everyone has a telephone. In addition, many people will not respond to an unknown voice. While this method is easy to administer, speedy and relatively inexpensive, it may tend to alienate potential respondents because of inconvenience at particular times. It is, however, a useful approach in **industrial** market research.

4. Panel data Members of a representative panel are selected, each member maintaining a diary of his relevant actions (e.g. which T.V. programmes were viewed). At the end of a specified time the diary is replaced by a new one. Panels are often used in consumer research for goods such as groceries – the housewife keeping a record of her purchases. The main advantage of the consumer panel is that it gives a continuous record of the buying patterns/habits of the same person as opposed to an *ad hoc* survey. Additionally, of course, information can be gathered quite quickly. This method is the only one which faithfully reveals the extent of **brand loyalty**. It is also occasionally used to determine the attitudes of distributors and wholesalers.

Questionnaire design
This is perhaps the most critical phase of the whole survey. The first point to bear in mind is:

What are you trying to determine?
A questionnaire is simply a tool for the collection of data from **potential informants**. The following points are relevant:

1. The informant's **co-operation** must be obtained and retained.

2. Communicate easily: no ambiguities; no unfamiliar words (in one survey, only 20% of the sample understood the word 'chronology'); no differing concepts (e.g. what is meant by 'good' or 'nice').

3. The informant must be allowed to work out **his** response – preferably with pre-coded answers (using prompt cards if necessary). It is often difficult to analyse **open-ended** answers.

Market research provides two basic types of information:

1. Qualitative, which gives an idea, an impression, and which may require only a few, in-depth, exploratory interviews.

2. Quantitative, which is far more definitive and on which the characteristics of a small sample are considered to be representative of those of a larger population.

Classification variables
Samples may be drawn from combinations such as the following:

1. Area Population, type, socio-economic groups, etc.
2. Accommodation Age, type, number of rooms, garage, rented, etc.
3. Household Size, structure, income, car owner, monocolour T.V., etc.
4. Sex
5. Age Under 15, 16–25, 26–35, 36–45, etc.
6. Marital status Married, single, divorced, widowed.
7. Education Secondary, tertiary, university, etc.
8. Socio-economic group A, B, C1, C2, D, E, e.g. Market research survey of:

  (a) South East; male, SEG A, B, C, under 35 or
  (b) West; female, SEG C1, C2, over 20.

Ideally, the questions should be capable of being answered quickly and easily:

1. Semantic scales

| Very good | Good | Satisfactory | Poor | Very poor |

or

2. Monopolar

Sweet ⟷ Not sweet

or

3. Bipolar

Sweet | | | | | | | Sour

← tendency to →

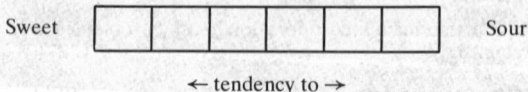

4.	Question	Answer	Code	Skip to question
1.	Have you ever had a meal at a Chinese restaurant?	Yes	1	2
		No	2	30
2.	When did you last eat in a Chinese restaurant?	Less than one week ago.	3	3
		Less than one month ago.	4	25
		More than one month ago.	5	28
3.	How often do you use a Chinese restaurant?	Every week.	1	4
		Every month.	2	34
		From time to time.	3	10

Obviously, the skip to questions must relate to the objectives of the survey. Question 30 might therefore read:

Question	Answer	Code	Skip to question
30. Why have you never had a meal at a Chinese restaurant?	Don't like Chinese food.	7	35
	Can't afford it.	8	38
	No Chinese restaurant nearby.	7	40

It is always sound practice to **pre-test** the questionnaire before using it on the sample population.

The boxes may be pre-coded with numerical values to allow for subsequent analysis, as might also a prompt card, e.g.:

5. Prompt card
Please read the following list of activities and select those **three** in which you participate most frequently:

Horse-riding	01	Visiting the pub	11
Sailing	02	Cricket	12
Football	03	Tennis	13
Golf	04	Rugby	14
Swimming	05	Squash	15
Gardening	06	Badminton	16
Watching T.V.	07	Visiting cinema	17
Ice-skating	08	Shooting	18
Bingo	09	Cycling	19
Bowling	10	Athletics	20

Skip instructions may be inserted in the questionnaire, especially if the survey is to be undertaken by personal interview.

SAMPLING

To be *statistically* reliable, a sample must be both large enough to be representative of the **total population** and proportionate, i.e. the percentages of various characteristics – such as SEG, sex, age – to be found in the total population must also be approximately the same in the sample population.

Types of sample

1. Random Each member of the population has a known and equal chance of being drawn from the total population available.

2. Systematic Drawing, say, every tenth member of a population.

3. Cluster A cluster of samples, say, in a block of flats, particularly where there is a widely dispersed population.

4. Quota The interviewer may be told to see/question a specified number of specifically named people in the above examples. To economize, the interviewer is given a **quota** to fill, i.e. interview a number of people in various categories or stratifications, such as males and/or by age and/or by socio-economic group. The main advantage of quota sampling is that associated costs may be considerably less.

Sampling should be tempered by considerations of cost and practicability.

Handling the information
How the information is processed will depend on what is being investigated or determined. In this chapter simple analysis will be dealt with. For more detailed methods the reader is referred to the companion books in this series, particularly *Statistics* and *Operational Research*.

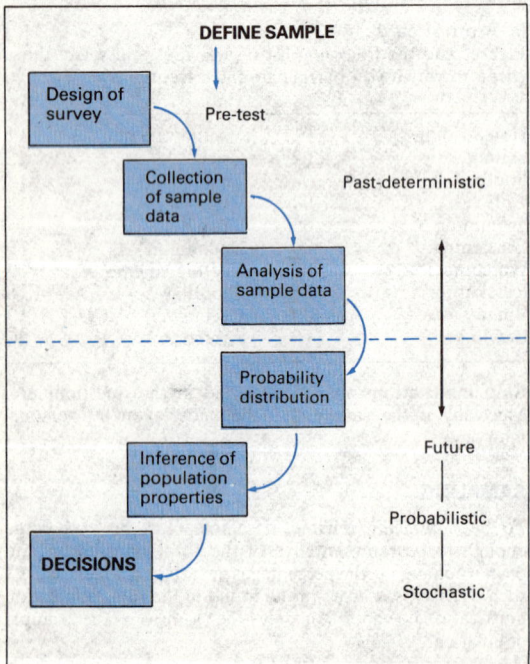

Figure 4. Representation of a statistical study

The chronology of the survey and the processing of the sampling information is shown in Figure 4.

The ordinary share index of the *Financial Times* is an example of the value and limitation of sampling. Its purpose is to show the *general trend* of equity prices, but, out of the thousands of individual stocks, only 30 representative leaders are selected. Its value is that it is a general indicator, *particularly* over a long period.

The task of the market researcher and/or statistician is to:

1. Measure accurately.

2. Couch problems in quantitative terms.

3. Prepare the ground for **logical inference**.

His fact-finding, however, does not supercede judgement – it is complementary.

Having obtained information from the population sample, what can be said or **inferred** from future or all the samples of population properties?

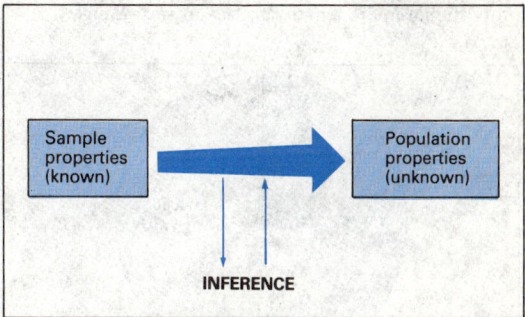

Figure 5. Inferential analysis

DATA PRESENTATION AND ANALYSIS

Raw data is that data which is recorded in the way or order in which it is obtained or in some other arbitrary fashion. This raw data is then **processed**. It must be organized into an easily understood format by using pictorial representations such as tables, graphs, bar charts or histograms in order that trends or particular patterns can be readily detected.

From this raw data, certain parameters may also be derived such as **the mean, the median** and **the mode**. It is also important that details of the survey are recorded at the time the data is collected: e.g. **Survey**: N.E. London; males, 20–40 years, SEG B, C1, C2.

Representation of data may be done by tabulation, graphically, by pie charts, pictograms, bar charts or histograms.

1. Pie charts
Example Customer attendance at a restaurant is given below.

Year	1977	1978	1979	1980	Total
No. attended	3000	4000	5500	7500	20000

(Frequency is the number of times something happened)

Year	Frequency	Relative frequency
1977	3000	$3000 \div 20000 = 0.150$
1978	4000	$= 0.200$
1979	5500	$= 0.275$
1980	7500	$= 0.375$
	20000	1.000

Represent this information as bisectors of a circle proportional in arc length (or area or sector angle).

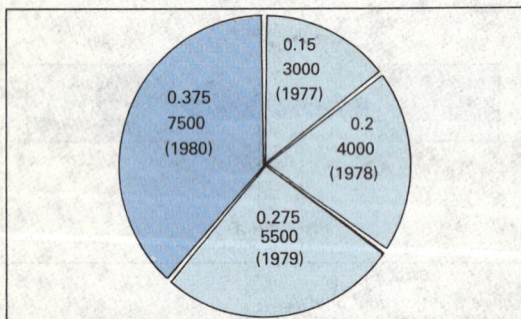

Figure 6. Pie chart representation

The pie chart gives a faithful representation as a proportion of observations but it may also give a misleading impression, e.g. by emphasizing a particular segment.

2. The histogram
This is a frequency diagram which is used to represent grouped data. The histogram consists of a number of rectangles, one rectangle corresponding to each **cell**, the **areas** of which represent the frequencies within the respective cells.

To each cell, defined by the data grouping, there corresponds a segment of the **variable** value axis. The vertical sides of the rectangles correspond to the cell **end-points**; the midpoints of the **bases** of the rectangles correspond to the **cell mid-point**.

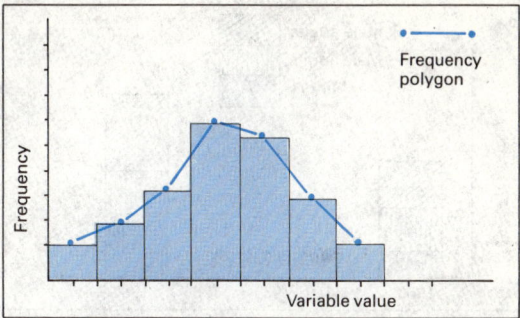

Figure 7. A histogram

If the cell widths are all equal then the histogram resembles a bar chart but if the cell widths vary then this similarity disappears.

3. Pictograms (ideograms), for example customer attendance.

Figure 8. A pictogram

Disadvantages Values of less than 1000 are not accurately represented. It is necessary to maintain a uniform **symbol** throughout to ensure fidelity.

4. Column charts
Multiple bar charts are used for the aggregates of observations or aggregated observations of similar factors, as shown in Figure 9, e.g. attendances at a cinema in one day.

	Minors	Male adults	Female adults	Total
1963	100	150	200	450
1967	250	150	300	700

This is represented in Figure 9 as shown.

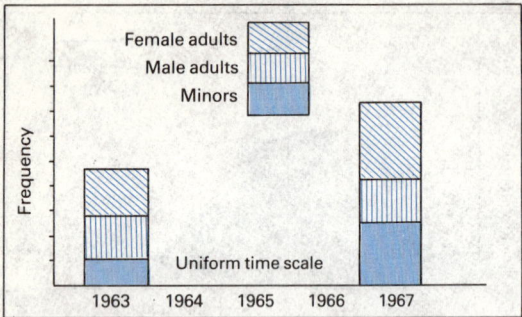

Figure 9. A column chart

5. Cumulative frequency diagrams

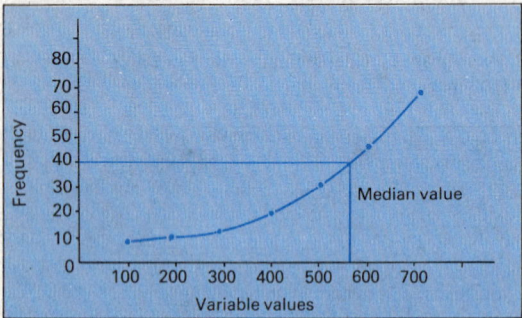

Figure 10. Cumulative frequency chart

The frequency of each **subsequent** variable value is added to the **previous** frequency to produce a cumulative frequency.

If a perpendicular is dropped at the half-way mark of the frequencies, then the point which is bisected on the horizontal axis **(the variable value)** is known as the **median**.

Measures of location
It is usual to determine the centre of the frequency distribution by using one of the following:

1. Arithmetical mean ($\bar{x}$).
2. The mode.
3. The median.

1. The mean (the common average)
x is the variable, e.g. number of runs scored.
$\sum$ (sigma) means 'the sum of'.
$\sum$x is the *sum* of all the variables.
n is the number of times the opportunity arose.

For example, in 5 innings a batsman scores 23, 15, 10, 49, 34 runs (total 131),

His mean score is $\dfrac{\sum x}{n} = \dfrac{131}{5} = 26$.

If he scores some of these values more than once, i.e. the variable becomes more frequent, then the mean $(\bar{x}) = \dfrac{\sum fx}{\sum f}$

Example

Number of runs	20 30 40 50 60 70 = x
Number of innings	1 2 3 2 2 1 = f

This can be represented as:

x	f	fx
20	1	20
30	2	60
40	3	120
50	2	100
60	2	120
70	1	70
	11	490

thus, $\bar{x} = \dfrac{\sum fx}{\sum f} = \dfrac{490}{11} = 44.5$

2. The mode is that value of a variable occurring with the **greatest** frequency, e.g. in the cricket scores the mode is **40**. The disadvantage of the mode is that only one value is expressed but it is more typical of a group than either the mean or the median. (Consider the manager of a shoe shop reordering his stock. When considering **shoe sizes** would he consider the mean, the median or the mode?)

3. The median is an example of a **partition** value. Consider data arranged in an ascending order of magnitude (of variable value), then the variable value associated with the *middle* observation of this array is said to be the **median** of the distribution, e.g. in the cricket scores, the median is also 40.

Comparison of mean and median
The **mean** is useful if totals are of interest in the observation. The **median** is useful when the distribution is **skew**. Skew values have a disproportionate influence on the mean values, as shown in Figure 11.

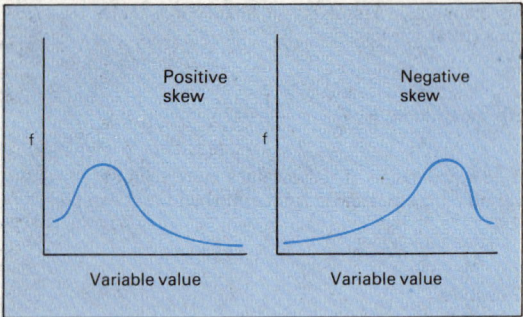

Figure 11. Skew distribution

Measures of dispersion
In the measures of location, for the sake of conciseness or for comparative purposes, a single figure was calculated to represent the whole group. Most market research studies are based on the assumption that the properties of a survey are **normally distributed** around the mean, i.e. there are proportionately as many *negative* phenomena as there are *positive* phenomena. For example, the number of runs *less* than the mean equals the number *more* than the mean.

It is often necessary to know how individual items in a group are dispersed around the mean. The smaller the figure for dispersion, the more compact is the group. The main measures of dispersion are:

1. Range This is the difference between the largest observed value and the smallest observed value, e.g. cricket scores, 70−20; range 50.

2. Standard deviation
Consider the following:

Output per hour	No. of workers
26	1
27	4
28	6
29	4
30	1

Graphically, this information is **normally** distributed as shown in Figure 12.

The curve is **symmetrical** about its mean; it is **bell-shaped**; it is a **normal** curve.

If any frequency distribution conforms to this pattern then the standard deviation (SD) in regard to such a distribution shows the following characteristics:

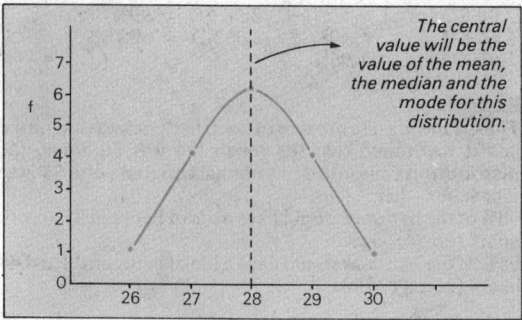

Figure 12. Normal distribution

2/3rds of such a group will lie within the range of one SD from the mean.
19/20ths of the group will lie within 2 SDs from the mean.

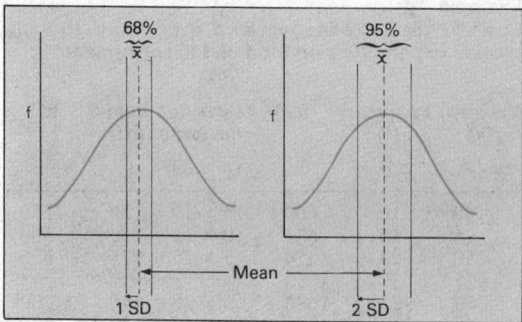

Figure 13. Standard deviation

More accurately, the area under the standard normal curve = 1.

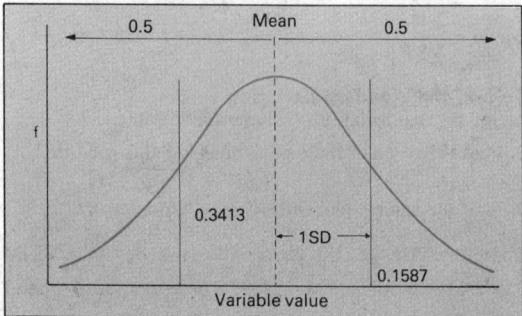

Figure 14. Standard deviation values

1.00 SD (or z) = 68.26%	2.58 SD = 99%
1.64 SD = 90%	3.00 SD = 99.75%
1.96 SD = 95%	

Example

Thus, if the life of a number of torch batteries was measured and it was found that the **mean life** was 36 hours, the **distribution** conformed to a normal curve and **one SD** was four hours, then:

68% of the batteries would have a life of between 32 and 40 hours (36±4).

95% of the batteries would have a life of between 28 and 44 hours (36±8 (2SD)).

To calculate the standard deviation

1. Find the deviations from the mean.
2. Square these deviations.
3. Find the mean of the sum of these deviations squared.
4. Find the square root of this mean.

Example

Consider the following tabulated data, which gives the **weekly expenditure on food of 130 consumers**.

Variable (x)	Frequency (f)	fx	Deviation from the mean (dxf)	fd2
£s A	B	C	D	E
40	10	400	15 × 10 = 150	2250
45	15	675	10 × 15 = 150	1500
50	25	1250	5 × 25 = 125	625
55	30	1650		
60	28	1680	5 × 28 = 140	700
65	13	845	10 × 13 = 130	1300
70	9	630	15 × 9 = 135	2025
	130	7130		8400

$$\text{Mean} = \frac{\sum fx}{\sum f} = \frac{7130}{130} = 55$$

To find the standard deviation

1. Square the deviations (column E) = 8400.

2. Find the mean of these deviations = $\frac{8400}{130}$ = 64.0.

3. Find the square root of this mean $\sqrt{64.0}$ = 8.00.

Therefore 1SD = £8.00. Then, 68% of the consumers spend £55 ± £8 on food, i.e. £47–£63; 95% of the consumers spend £55 ± £16 on food, i.e. £39–£71. (All figures are rounded up for ease of calculation.)

To summarize

The mean $(\bar{x}) = \dfrac{\sum fx}{\sum f}$

Standard deviation $(z) = \sqrt{\dfrac{\sum fd2}{\sum f}}$.

In practice, normal distribution tables have been determined which give the areas under the normal curve, as a proportion of the total area, between the mean and a point (above the mean) expressed as a number of standard deviations.

Extract of normal distribution table

Z	.00	.01	.02	.03	.04	.05	.06	.07	.08	.09
0.1	.0398	.0438	.0478	.0517	.0557	.0596	.0636	.0675	.0714	.0753
0.5	.1915	.1950	.1985	.2019	.2054	.2088	.2123	.2157	.2190	.2224
1.0	.3413	.3438	.3461	.3485	.3508	.3531	.3554	.3577	.3599	.3621
1.5	.4332	.4345	.4357	.4370	.4382	.4394	.4406	.4418	.4429	.4441
2.0	.4772	.4778	.4783	.4788	.4793	.4798	.4803	.4808	.4812	.4817

Worked example

Sweets are automatically packed for the retail trade in boxes containing 6 kilograms (kg). The packing machine is set for 6 kg but there is a standard deviation of 0.05 kg. Calculate the probability that a box of sweets selected at random will weigh less than 5.9 kg.

Solution

The mean weight is 6 kg, as shown in Figure 15.

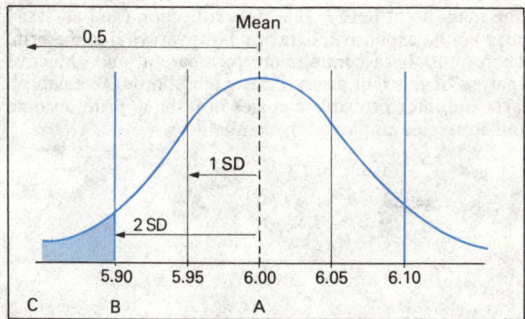

Figure 15. Worked example — sweets

5.90 kg (B) is 2SD from the mean.
From tables 2SD = 0.4772
From C to A   = 0.5
Therefore, from C to B = 0.5 − 0.4772 = 0.0228 (less than 5.9 kg).

Therefore, the probability that a box of sweets will weigh *less* than 5.9kg *is* 0.0228 (or 2.28%) (there is, of course, a similar probability that a box of sweets will weigh *more* than 5.9kg).

In this chapter, only a broad hint of the scale and scope of market research has been given for there are several excellent and detailed texts on the subject. In essence, marketing research should be an important feature of any enterprise for without information the firm is impotent. The data gathered are essential to short-term **tactical** planning and for determining long-term **strategies**, and most of the data can be obtained free of charge. For example, the following type of analysis is readily available to any firm from central government sources or from the banking sector, both of which employ statisticians and economic analysts.

> **Between 1965 and 1975** a greater proportion of consumer **income** has been spent on luxuries such as holidays and durable goods.
>
> In 1965 consumer expenditure on **food** amounted to 21% of income. In 1975 only 18% of expenditure was on food. Expenditure on **alcohol** rose from 6% to 9%. Since a wide range of SEGs have gained access to credit facilities more expensive consumer **durables** have been purchased, e.g. the sale of radio and electrical goods increased by 88%.
>
> The sale of convenience foods increased dramatically while the sale of bread and cereals declined by 10%. There has been a 165% rise in the sale of **sports** equipment. Holidays abroad have increased by 45% (and so on) *(Barclay's Review)*.

The main point here is that data collection (and analysis) need not be expensive; data are, however, vital to the firm. There must be a commitment to a careful and objective analysis of relevant areas of research in order to establish facts and infer probable changes in fashion, taste, income and strategies employed by competitors.

Chapter 3

Consumer Buying Behaviour

NEEDS AND MOTIVATION

CONSUMPTION is a function of:

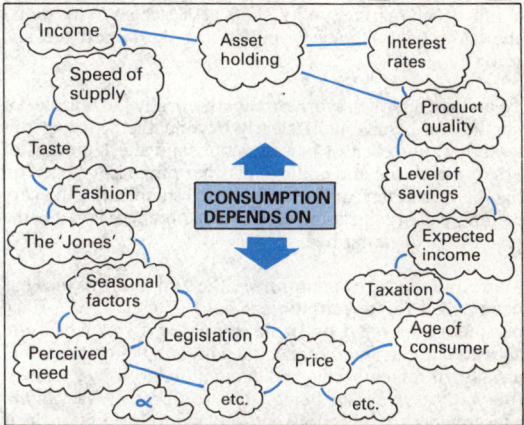

Figure 16. Aspects of consumption

There are many factors which persuade or stimulate a consumer to purchase a product or service and Figure 16 illustrates just a few of these factors.

> If it is possible to understand and then predict the way in which individuals are motivated it might be possible to influence or change the components of the motivating package in order to achieve the firm's short-term and long-term objectives – but would that constitute efficient management or effective manipulation? (Paraphrased from *Understanding Organizations* by C. Handy.)

Can x motivate y or merely offer y the opportunity to possess certain factors which y considers important? x motivates y and y is motivated by x, but is x an object or a person? Is x money, hunger, status, power . . . or what?

Human behaviour is a complex process which is exceedingly difficult to define or simulate for there is a multiplicity of variables which do not allow for relatively simple models to describe it adequately. Whereas physical laws are comparatively stable over a period of time, the inter-relationships of those factors which govern and determine human behaviour are highly dynamic and may change significantly in a short space of time. In attempting to understand consumer purchasing behaviour and patterns, it is apparent that an understanding of individual **motivation** is also necessary.

Consider a housewife who purchases a medium-sized tub of soft margarine such as Blue Band from Tesco's. She has made several decisions, and to Tesco's and the manufacturers of Blue Band her decisions are very important – they are also important to their competitors. Why did she buy Blue Band? Why not Stork margarine? Why did she not buy butter? Why a soft margarine? Why a tub of margarine? Why shop at Tesco's? Why didn't she try to save money by purchasing the largest tub and so on?

To analyse and then synthesize methodically the reasons for her buying behaviour is clearly beyond the scope of this textbook, but each of her decisions, and the hundreds of others which she and millions of other purchasers made on that particular day, are of fundamental significance to every commercial organization. However, a purchase is rarely the result of a *single* motive.

Man is influenced by many forces, the sum total of which has been called the **psychological field** (Engel, 1968). Each person is motivated by **basic needs** or drives which are activated in the *present* time, but a human being is capable, usually, of remembering and being influenced by events of the *past* as well as being able to forecast the *future* consequences of his actions and behaviour. In addition, he is greatly influenced by his **environment** and particularly the **social role** of others. There will be a number of factors which determine his ultimate behaviour and some of these factors may well conflict. The final behaviour, therefore, is the result of many complex inputs.

There are a number of theories of motivation, some specific to a work situation but others less specific in their application. There does appear to be a general consensus among behavioural scientists that individuals will exhibit specific behavioural patterns when such behaviour results in the fulfilment of an **objective**, the attainment of which ultimately satisfies a **need**. There are two basic kinds of need, firstly, the **physiological**, i.e. biogenic (such as the need for food, sleep, sex and physical comfort), and secondly, **psychological**, i.e. psychogenic (such as status, recognition, acceptance and achievement). The best known of need theories is, perhaps, that of Abraham Maslow who postulated a hierarchy of needs, the lower order ones having to be satisfied before the higher order needs could be activated.

The first four stages are fairly easy to understand but the final step is more complex and of this Maslow says, '. . .this tendency might be phrased as the desire to become more and more what one idiosyncratically is, to become everything that one is **capable** of becoming. . .' (Maslow, 1943).

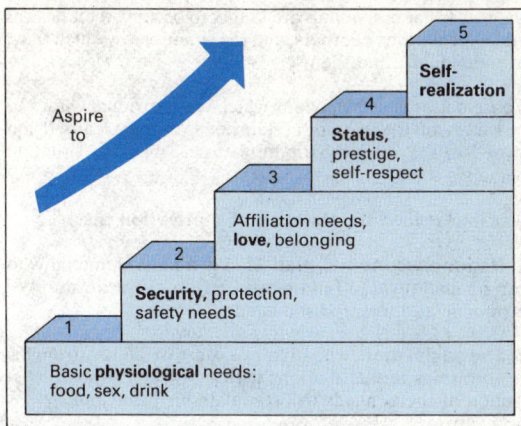

Figure 17. The hierarchy of needs

There is an overall tendency for the series of needs to appear in a *sequence* of domination. The lower order needs are satisfied primarily through **economic (purchasing)** behaviour but the higher ones are satisfied through **symbolic** behaviour of a psychological or social content. All behaviour is multi-motivated but a number of writers have placed the notion of **self-actualization**, or a similar concept, in a central position. To pursue one's individual goals or potential, however, requires an element of disregard for the remainder of *society* – one of the more influential of the behavioural determinants. Social life requires *conforming* conduct; the rules of society are learned through **socialization** and when tempted to depart from the rules **or norms**, in order to fulfil a need, the individual is constrained by the fact that others in his social group value these norms and are prepared to support their beliefs about what is right with *sanctions*. Thus, it is through the use of shared norms, supported by sanctions, that *predictable* patterns of social interaction arise and are maintained. An understanding of this phenomenon makes it easier to appreciate the tendency of consumers to 'keep up with the Jones' and to maintain a standard of living which is commensurate with the socio-economic group or class to which the consumer aspires or *believes* himself to belong. A renowned sociologist, Robert Merton, argues that members of the lower classes are the ones most likely to *innovate* – to seek success by resorting to illegitimate means. Members of the lower middle class are more likely to become *ritualists* – to abandon the pursuit of success as fruitless and to become entrenched in the *rules* of their social class.

Children tend to perpetuate the norms of their socio-economic group. These groupings are a major determinant of human behaviour and are governed, to a large degree, by the **roles** that individuals are taught to occupy, their desires and expectations of others, and the situations in which they, as individuals, find themselves.

Those patterns of behaviour which the individual *knows* to be successful in satisfying certain needs become learned and stored in the memory for future use, when the situation demands them.

Schein classified the **theories of motivation** thus:

1. Rational/economic man Man is a passive animal who can be manipulated (and motivated) by the acquisition of economic and materialistic needs.

2. The social man, who obtains a sense of identity from his relationships and affiliations with others and whose satisfaction of social needs will stimulate his behaviour.

3. Self-actualizing man, who seeks psychological maturity and aspires to be an individual and to control his own destiny. Motivated by his inner self.

4. Complex man, who is incredibly variable for he has many needs to satisfy, some of which will conflict and will lead to *optimization* of need satisfaction.

It will be appreciated that motivation and the resulting exhibited behaviour are complex processes. This complexity is compounded when an individual's needs or aspirations are blocked for some reason.

In 1939 a group of Yale psychologists formulated **the frustration–aggression** hypothesis. **Frustration** was defined as the blocking of a motivated, goal-directed sequence of behaviour. Failure to attain the goal may lead to frustration which in turn may give way to **aggression** which manifests itself through the use of **defensive mechanisms**. Any defence mechanism is an attempt to reduce the tension associated with the non-attainment of a need. The more common of these mechanisms are depicted in Figure 18.

An explanation of some of these mechanisms may be necessary:

1. Displacement The emotions attached to one object are displaced onto another, e.g. boss reprimands employee; employee takes it out on his wife; wife punishes child. Another, more subtle form, is when individuals, particularly in groups, talk about broad, impersonal issues or the motives of others rather than focusing on their own personal feelings.

2. Rationalization is the act of offering socially acceptable excuses for what one wants to do when these reasons are not the real reasons, i.e. a sort of mechanism which allows people to live comfortably with their consciences.

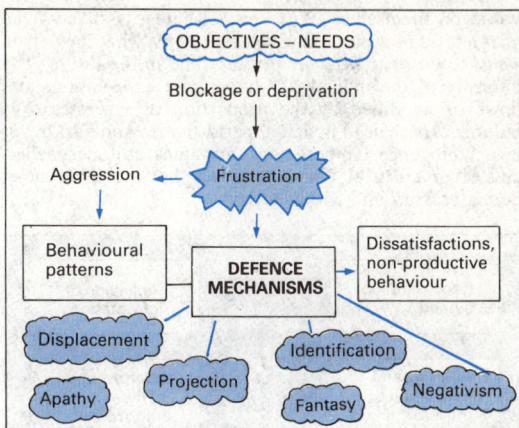

Figure 18. Defence mechanisms

3. Identification Imitation of someone else, particularly a superior or a member of a socially superior group, i.e. status and ego inflation.

4. Negativism Basically, resistance to change when such a change may reduce an individual's attainment of a need.

An individual's need deficiencies are often compensated for by his day-dreams **(fantasy)** in which he is always the central figure. The more a person's ego is denied satisfaction in real life, the more it will tend to find satisfaction in day-dreams. Rose Fyleman summed it up in her verse:

I've got such a heap of wishes
I've only said a few
I wish that I could wake some morning
And find they'd all come true.

There is no single or simple factor which will stimulate a purchase, for the action of buying a product occurs as a result of many inter-related, always complex and often conflicting forces. The components of the marketing mix – the product, its price, the method of promotion, the packaging and the point-of-sale outlet – and their correct permutation may not only initiate a buying pattern but, more importantly, may reinforce *preconceived* purchasing plans. A housewife may decide to buy margarine but which type, how much and which brand may not be settled until she arrives at the supermarket. It is appropriate to remind the reader of the basic decision-making model which applies as much to purchasing decisions as to any other activity. Even **impulse purchasing** follows a decision-making format (Figure 19).

Individuals have an **image** of themselves and also put a

value on themselves. With this self-image and self-value goes a level of aspiration which represents what the person *wants* to do or to *become* at some time in the future. The intensity of the individual's hopes and expectations are, however, modified by the proportion of successes over failures experienced in actual performance and also by his own intelligence, temperament and values, attitudes, beliefs and other **cultural characteristics** that are inherent at home, at work and within society.

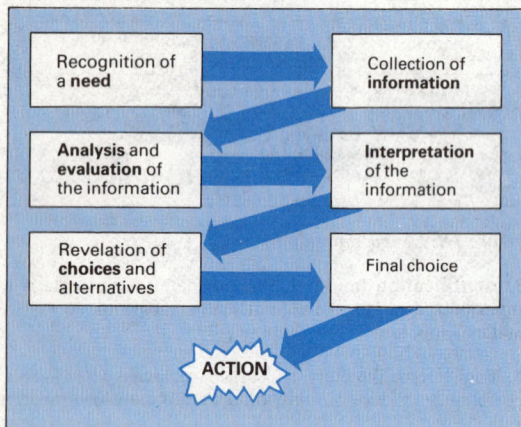

Figure 19. Consumer decision-making process

Socio-economic groups

An understanding of need satisfaction is fundamental to an understanding of behaviour, and the need hypothesis can be extrapolated to include and predict actual and potential purchasing patterns. Other factors are also important including **perception** (Chapter 5), the influence of **family life**, particularly which member influences the buying decisions, **status reinforcement** and **social expectations**. In this latter context, it is no longer adequate or commercially acceptable to categorize consumers only in terms of broad social class structure such as upper, middle and lower classes, for such classification is far too imprecise and nebulous. Instead, a definitive segmentation has arisen, namely the concept of **socio-economic groups** which classifies people according to their similarity of income, occupation and education as delineated by the National Readership Survey. A precis of the groups and their characteristics is tabulated on page 41.

Members of the same SEG exhibit certain *similarities* in their expectations, values and behaviours and will tend to give different priorities to the satisfaction of their needs compared with members of another group. Clearly, however, this classification is by no means rigid. Over-lapping of membership will occur with some members of the

Socio-economic group	Type of occupation	Example
A	Higher managerial administrative, professional.	Dental surgeon, senior officer in the forces, owner of large business.
B	Intermediate managerial.	Surveyor, bank manager.
C1	Supervisory or clerical managerial.	Bank clerk, SRN, estate agent, teacher.
C2	Skilled manual workers.	Foreman, welder, junior NCO.
D	Semi-skilled and unskilled.	Porter, driver, postman.
E	Those at lowest level of subsistence.	Casual workers, state pensioners.

low SEGs actually earning more than members of high SEGs; **ego and status inflation** resulting from reference group influences will tend to occur, but, as a method of segmentation, the grouping is very important.

Market segmentation also attempts to differentiate consumers according to such characteristics or classifications as age, sex, ethnic group, religion and geographical location. In recent years, other, less definitive, classifications have arisen such as *ambitiousness* and *price-sensitivity*. Through an awareness of market segments, the marketing management can develop an effective **launch campaign** and total sales method by aiming the advertising, promotion and product image at a specific segment and modifying the marketing approach to meet the requirements of each segment or combination of segments.

ASPECTS OF CONSUMPTION

Consumer purchasing behaviour is influenced not only by cultural, social and psychological factors but also by economic effects. The whole economic system is motivated by wants. To an economist, **demand** for a product is *want* accompanied by an *ability to pay* for a good at a given price.

The nature of demand
Goods wanted for short-term or immediate satisfaction are known as **consumer goods**, e.g. a house, or a suit, but products which are required for intermediate consumption or use in the manufacture of other products are known as producers' or **capital goods**. Consumer goods may be

durable or **non-durable**. Durable goods can be used over a period of time, e.g. furniture, clothes. Non-durable goods are consumed at once, e.g. a visit to the theatre or a glass of milk.

A product (or service) is said to have **utility**, i.e. it can satisfy a want; it is this utility which is the link between the product and the consumer. However, the utility of a product **diminishes** as the amount of that commodity increases because there is a limit to the desire for a particular product. This phenomenon is known as the law of **Diminishing Marginal Utility**. Demand will also be influenced by other factors including:

1. The consumer's **scale of preferences** and his willingness to substitute product A for his sacrifice of product B.

2. Complementary products, i.e. as the sale of one product increases, so might the sale of another, e.g. nuts and bolts, strawberries and cream.

3. Price equilibrium and the law of demand, i.e. the demand for a particular product will fall as the price rises.

4. The proportion of **discretionary income** available, i.e. the consumer may spend non-essential income at his discretion. A change in **fiscal** policy which increases direct taxation may affect his discretionary income: so might a change in government **monetary policy**, e.g. an increase in the cost of borrowing interest rates.

5. Elasticity of demand The demand for some products changes very little even when there is a considerable increase in price, e.g. tobacco and bread. However, when there is a significant change in demand as a result of a small change in price, demand is said to be **elastic**. When there is little or no change in demand as a result of price changes, demand is said to be **inelastic**; its significance for the firm is that, where demand is elastic, a rise in price may result in falling revenue as a consequence of lost sales. Demand tends to be elastic when **substitute products** are readily available or when the purchase can be postponed, e.g. a pair of shoes, or when the product may be considered to be non-essential, e.g. a cinema outing. **Promotional elasticity** often occurs when demand for a product may be altered significantly by the extent and effectiveness of advertising and promotional campaigns.

6. Company or product reputation and pre- or post-purchase advice and **service** facilities will influence buying behaviour.

(For a more detailed analysis see *Economics*, in this series.)

Chapter 4

Corporate Objectives and Planning

THE OBJECTIVES

The objective(s) of an organization is seldom stated explicitly. A UK company incorporated under the Companies Act has a constitution called the **Memorandum** and **Articles** of Association but nowhere is the objective stated. The activities in which the firm may engage are listed under the Objects clause but these are not the objectives. In other words, what is it that the company, as a corporate body, wishes to achieve? – what are its goals? Although the firm has a *legal identity,* it is, of course, composed of many groups or **stakeholders**, including the investors or owners, which usually means that the ordinary shareholders and these other groups have nothing in common except their financial interest. To some extent, then, the company's *primary* objective must be related to this *financial* interest.

The individual shareholder's objective must be to maximize the **net present value** of his future cash flows, bearing in mind his tax position and whether he seeks *capital* growth with its inherent risks or a steady *income* in the form of dividends.

The more successful the board of directors is in achieving, say, a profit-maximization objective the better will their position be to satisfy the ordinary shareholder's aspirations, whatever profit distribution policy the board finally adopts. It is to the *ordinary* shareholders that the directors are accountable and therefore profit must be based on *ordinary shareholders' funds* and not on the total capital employed by the firm. However, the managing director of the company is accountable to the board and his objectives may be related to the **total capital** available to him, whether in the form of loans, preference shares or ordinary shares, in order to recommend expansion, diversification, exporting or meet a competitive challenge. Yet his yardstick of efficiency can still be measured in terms of profit, but related to the total capital employed. In addition, he has under his control the primary source of **revenue**, namely sales, and the expenditure in the **costs** associated with marketing, production, administration, etc. If he does not have both these variables, revenue and costs, under his control, he cannot measure his achievement of objectives in *profit* terms. Thus, in the functionally structured organization where the departmental managers are each in charge of a function such as marketing, personnel, production, etc. none of them can have an objective in terms of profit because not one of them has authority over both sales and production.

The production manager may, for example, have the

objective of producing orders at least cost; the marketing manager's target might be to achieve a 2% increase in market share. These objectives are different from the managing director's but are nevertheless contributory to it. It becomes apparent, then, that a **hierarchy of objectives** usually exists within the enterprise. Ideally, individual managers will attempt to achieve the pre-determined, organizationally defined **sub-system goal**. When he has to make judgements or use his discretion in the accomplishment of his tasks, the manager makes these judgements against the criterion of his objective. It follows, therefore, that he can only have *one primary objective,* for an objective can be defined as the criterion which determines the establishment of priorities between alternative (and conflicting) uses of resources. The factors which limit the extent to which individual managers and the organization can achieve their goals are called **constraints** – an additional objective would act simply as an additional constraint against achieving the primary objective.

THE PLANNING

In order to achieve an objective, **a plan** or series of sub-optimum plans is required. In addition to market research and the utilization of relevant information, events of the *past* must also influence the decision-making of *today* in order to determine the plans for *tomorrow*. Therefore, **corporate planning** is a necessary process which all organizations, however small, must undertake whether they do so formally or informally.

Argenti (1964) says that:

> Corporate planning. . .is a systematic and disciplined study designed to help to:
> **1. Identify** the **objectives** of the firm.
> **2.** Determine an appropriate **target**.
> **3.** Decide upon suitable **constraints**.
> **4.** Devise a practical **plan**.

It is difficult to advance a standard approach to corporate planning because of the variety of companies, their individual idiosyncrasies, and their diverse markets, products and inter-relationships. What might be considered sound strategical and tactical planning for one company may possibly be the antithesis for another firm in another market with a different product. Even so, the basic principles of corporate planning are common to all organizations.

Why bother to plan?
There are several basic reasons, all of which might be objectives, but in a commercial enterprise **adding value** and realizing that value in the form of **optimum profits** must remain the primary objective. Other reasons include:

1. To ensure **survival**.
2. To compete **cost effectively** and efficiently.

3. To **expand** – horizontally or laterally.
4. To **motivate** employees.
5. To discharge the firm's **social responsibilities**.

Corporate planning, however, like most activities, has disadvantages as well as merits:

Advantages
1. It provides for **delegation** of action.
2. It provides the bases for **managerial control** and co-ordination.
3. Economies and **cost minimization** can often be achieved.
4. **Mistakes** or potential hazards can be **minimized/** eliminated.
5. It provides for **purposeful** and deliberate **action**.
6. It prepares the groundwork for **individual** as well as departmental management by **objectives**.
7. **Diverging work** (and targets) can be avoided.

Disadvantages
1. It is **time-consuming** and expensive.
2. The drafted plan, once established, becomes relatively **inflexible** and may be difficult to modify.
3. Forecasting is always fraught with uncertainty and there is, therefore, an **element of risk**.
4. It may be difficult to obtain a **consensus** of agreement.

Despite the obvious disadvantages, planning remains the most *basic* of all managerial functions. This is because it involves selection, from many alternative courses of action, both for the total system and its environmental interaction, and for each sub-system within that enterprise. In order to be successful, the corporate plans require **implementation and action** otherwise any actions become simply a series of uncoordinated and random activities. Ideally, an overall objective – and certainly sub-system targets – should be defined in **quantifiable** terms in order that levels of attainment can be measured. Therefore the objectives must be cast in terms of:

1. *Purpose* Why are we doing it?
2. *Timing* When are we going to do it/achieve it?
3. *Resources* What are we going to use to do it with?

There will inevitably be many constraints which will limit the fulfilment of the plans. All of the stakeholders – the equity holders, the employees, the customers, the community and the government – have an interest in the firm and the overall objective, but their **sectional goals** may often take precedence. For example, the objectives of, say, the production manager might be to:

1. Achieve long production runs.
2. Sustain production at or above a certain level.
3. Achieve low production costs.
4. Maintain a stable number of employees and associated expertise.

On the other hand, a customer will be more interested in the product and its quality, quantity, availability, lead time, price and after-sales service.

In order to serve the interests of all – and therefore *optimize* profits – information about all stakeholders, both external and internal, is necessary. Unfortunately, information is often deficient in two ways. Firstly, information can never be complete and, since all decisions are taken about the future, there will always be doubt and *uncertainty*. Secondly, the firm may be unable or incapable of collecting the information it requires – partly because information is expensive to collect – or of making use of it, even if it does get the information.

Even when plans are made there still needs to be a varying degree of **control** in order to ensure that such plans are implemented effectively and correctly. It has been said that planning and control are the Siamese twins of management: a firm separates them at its peril, yet the more control is imposed, the less trust there can be, for **control** and **trust** are inversely proportional; the final mix determines the degree of **delegation** which is ultimately afforded.

So far in this chapter, we have discussed the use of the available information, attempted to reconcile the interested parties and formulated the broad objectives. The organizational objective must now be translated into more specific sub-system goals. Let us take, for example, a manufacturing company: its broad objective may perhaps be to concentrate upon the major product line and become world-wide distributors in that field.

Its sub-system goals might be to:

1. Raise long-term **finance** by equity rather than loans because the firm might wish to use risk capital.
2. Strengthen the **marketing** effort and sales force/agencies in, say, Latin America, Australia and the USA.
3. Allow for the **production**/manufacturing of some components by local labour and enterprise.
4. Dispose of those **product lines** which are not closely related to the major product.
5. Acquire manufacturing facilities in, say, EEC countries and Japan.

Those organizationally imposed sub-goals, which are quantifiable, can be controlled more easily but vague hopes and aspirations are useless as measures of attainment. In addition, quantifiable goals can be budgeted for and deadlines built into the operational and tactical plans. In other words, realistic **short-term targets** can be set and established as steps towards the more ideal **long-run objectives**, but it is important to distinguish between hopes and expectations.

In **corporate development**, there are four major areas in

which the establishment of objectives and comprehensive and formal planning are necessary:

1. Developing the existing business by, say, market penetration; defining the feasible options and the resources which will be required; and forecasting the possible financial results – in the form of net revenue – which might arise.

2. Developing an armoury of new activities unrelated to the current product line, i.e. total diversification preceded by detailed project analysis, including strengths and weaknesses.

3. Developing a combined portfolio by combining new activities with current products and services, e.g. by developing complementary products.

4. Development strategy by planning to acquire the capabilities and resources necessary to allow for integration and/or diversification.

Corporate planning is an attempt to chart and navigate the course of the company/organization, to formulate and develop its future strategy, and to detail the implementation of its tactical and operational plans. It achieves this by producing **short-term** and **long-term** objectives. The objectives, however, must be more than mere aspiration levels: they must be fully thought through and stated in quantified, operational terms.

However, once formulated, objectives do tend to be stable (although reviewed to meet changing conditions), mainly because there is little time available for all the coalition members of the planning committee to alter or re-draft the objectives. However, there are organizational factors which also affect the **decision-making process**, the most important of which include:

1. The **management style** and receptiveness, e.g. R. Likert's (1964) analysis is pertinent:
    (a) System I   – autocratic.
    (b) System II   – benevolent dictatorship.
    (c) System III – consultative.
    (d) System IV – participative.
(See *Organization Theory* in this series.)
2. The degree of **specialization** and the way in which work and labour are divided.
3. The extent to which the organization is **centralized** or decentralized.
4. The number of strata in the **hierarchy of authority** and the associated bureaucracy
5. The effectiveness of formal (and informal) **communication nets**.
6. The availability and responsiveness of the individual and group **decision-makers**.

Chapter 5

Communications

It is vital for any organization, through its members, to communicate effectively both **internally** between the various grades of employees and **externally** between its members (i.e. the organization) and its actual and potential customers. No sub-system of a commercial enterprise is likely to have as much dialogue with these customers as that of the marketing department. If the fundamental mechanics of the communication process can be understood, it may be possible to isolate faults in or improve an existing system. Clearly, the external effectiveness of the communication process is an integral part of the **promotional** aspects of the marketing mix.

A number of experiments have shown conclusively that:

1. If the communication can first arouse the recipient's **needs** and then present information that tends to *satisfy* those needs, the information will be accepted more readily.

2. Attitudes change *more* when communications which are actually *wanted* by the recipient are presented first, followed by the less desirable ones, than when the less desirable ones are presented first.

3. In a discussion or argument, the *for–against* sequence is more effective than the *against–for* order.

There are three basic forms of communication:

1. Verbal (or aural, including, say, music).
2. Written (or drawn, including, say, paintings/sketches).
3. Body language.

THE COMMUNICATION PROCESS

All communication has a **source** who initiates the activity and is often referred to as the **changer**, for he will only communicate if he hopes to bring about some change of attitude, action or thought in a **recipient** (the changee).

The source will invariably respond to the recipient's reaction, i.e. the **feedback**. This will take the form of stimuli which are received by one or more of the five senses, principally, of course, visual and aural (but occasionally tactile).

How the recipient or changee responds depends on a number of interrelating factors, the most important of which are his **perceptive** ability and his inherent attitudes, which are formulated by his own peculiar **values** and **beliefs**. These, in turn, are influenced by the culture of his present and past environments, his education, status, personality, etc. The interaction of these variables is shown in Figure 20.

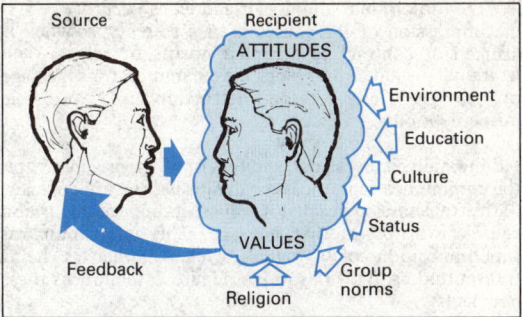

Figure 20. Communication interaction

How the listener **perceives** the actual communication can also significantly affect his attitude and subsequent response. For example, the esteem in which the source is held, his style of dress, his personality, his objectives, his apparent credibility – all of these may influence the effectiveness of the communicator.

Unfortunately, people tend to **stereotype** people: 'I don't

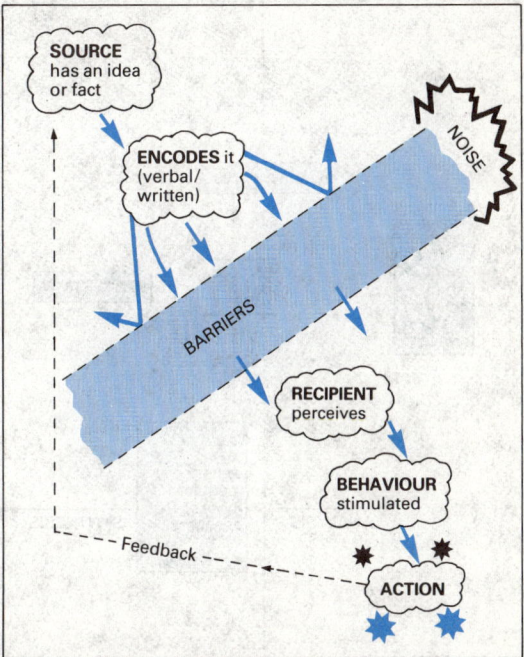

Figure 21. Model of communication process

like the **look** of him'; 'long hair and jeans'; 'shifty eyes'. If the impression of the source is of a stereotype which is disliked or contrary to accepted **norms** or values, then irrational prejudice may block the communicator's message or, at the least, cause **distortion** and probable misperception.

Additionally, if any signal, auditory or otherwise, interrupts the communication process or diminishes the effectiveness of the transmission because it reduces its impact, it may also cause distortion of that message. This interruption or superimposition of a signal, while another is being transmitted, is known as **noise**. Figure 21 embraces these new facts.

The feedback (which itself may be affected by noise) stimulates the source (or *actor*) to respond to his *audience* in an appropriate manner. The source learns how to improve his ability to communicate more effectively by modifying his code, e.g. the language he employs or by changing his channel of communication. The feedback or responsiveness of the recipient can also be interpreted by observing the recipient's posture.

Both the recipient and the source react (behave) according

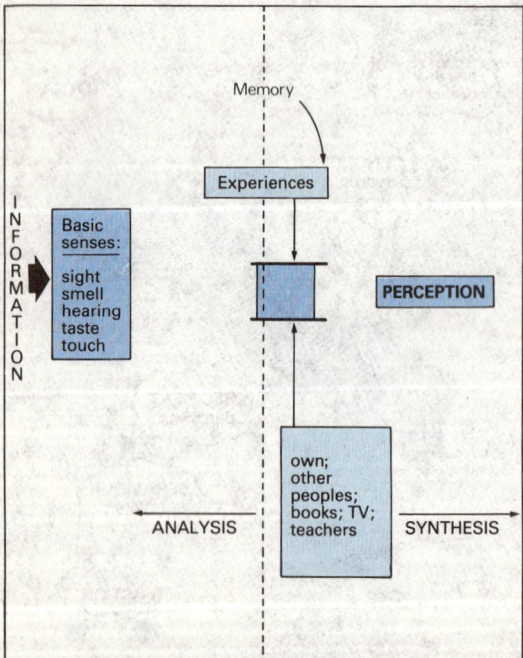

Figure 22. The perception process

to their perception of the message and the prevailing circumstances. The communication in either direction is often reinforced by gestures and/or body movements. The **perception** process, much simplified, consists of the reception of information by the basic senses and the modification of that information by **experiential** learning and resulting behaviour. This process is shown in Figure 22.

Sometimes the senses are fooled or the experiences may be incomplete, in which case the ultimate perception may be wrong. Reality is not necessarily what is sensed. However, if a situation is **perceived** as real, the resulting **behaviour** will be real in its *consequences*. This phenomenon has a significant contribution to make to the promotional tactics of the firm.

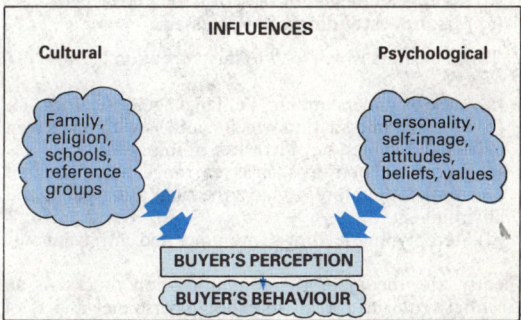

Figure 23. Cultural influences

The accuracy of the message is increased significantly, because of the nature and importance of the feedback mechanism in stimulating an appropriate response, when both parties can observe the gestures, the facial and/or body movements (or even the physical touch) of the other party. In 1966, Edouard Jouard'd observed couples seated at restaurant tables and counted the number of times a couple found it necessary to touch each other while talking. The average frequency of contact in one hour was as follows:

City	No. of times
San Juan	180
Paris	110
Gainsville (USA)	2
London	0

The communication process can be considered successful only when the recipient has both correctly understood the message and has taken the action which the communicator wished to stimulate. He must, of course, have overcome the major barriers to communicating. These are:

1. Wrong **source** and/or recipient.
2. Basic **facts** wrong.
3. Wrong **timing**.
4. Wrong **code**-language, non-verbal.
5. Prejudice/entrenched attitudes.
6. Noise leading to misperception, inappropriate behaviour, wrong action.

Barriers, which are relevant to the person for whom the message is intended, include:

1. Those barriers which prevent subsequent action because of:

(a) Lack of **motivation** by the recipient.
(b) **Inexperience** and/or lack of basic knowledge.
(c) **Misunderstanding** of the message.

2. Those barriers which lead to misperception because of:

(a) Lack of understanding, i.e. language difficulties.
(b) Ignoring information which conflicts with one's own beliefs and values, i.e. **filtration** of information.
(c) **Emotional** barriers such as fear, anger and distrust; it is essential, therefore, to have the right atmosphere and environment.
(d) Stereotyping, leading to prejudice and entrenchment.

Clearly, the theory of the communication process is an essential requisite for all marketing personnel and is of particular significance when determining the *advertising* campaign, but it is also important to remember that the success or failure of any message depends on many factors other than the purely rational ones or the degree of attention which the message actually receives.

Communication within the organization

An individual is dependent upon, and indeed limited by, his ability to send, receive and interpret communications. An organization is similarly placed. External communication has already been mentioned but it is also necessary to consider the communication process *within* the enterprise. If a biological analogy is used, the significance of this internal communication is readily appreciated. By transmitting impulses along nerve channels and by using chemical messengers, the sub-systems within the body can be instructed to vary or modify performance or to act in a specific manner which, in a healthy individual, protects the integrity of the sub-system in particular and the body as a whole. The failure of a sub-system, such as the cardiovascular system, to respond to these stimuli may seriously endanger the organism and threaten its continued existence. Compare a commercial enterprise with its sub-systems – personnel, finance, production, etc. and their various sub-divisions – with that of the human body. The enterprise has a *nerve centre* which issues instructions, and the sub-systems react and ideally produce feedback to the nerve centre to let it know that it has responded or otherwise. If high-power magnification is used, the sub-system will be seen to consist of **groups** and within the groups, **individuals**. Between all of these – individuals, groups, sub-divisions, sub-systems, departments, etc. – there must be an **effective** (and efficient) communication process. Patterns of communication do develop and the channels for the flow of messages become established and formalized. These channels are usually known as communications networks. Informal patterns of communication (the grapevine) also develop (discussed more fully in the *Organization Theory* book in this series).

The structure of the formal communication nets are often depicted as in Figure 24. A, B, C, D and E may be individuals, groups or even departments.

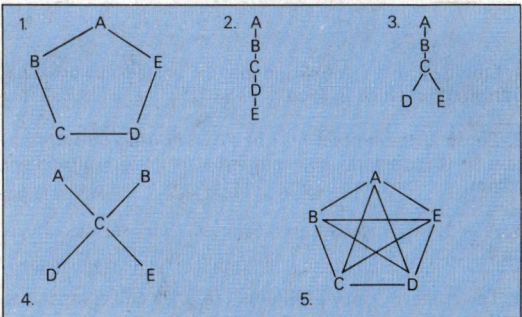

Figure 24. Formal communication nets

It will be seen that all the members (or groups) within these nets are linked but often with mediators interposed. So, in net (1), **A** may communicate directly with **B** and **E** but not with **C** and **D** so that a relay system of communication is necessary and, to a greater or lesser extent, such a relay system is also necessary in nets (2), (3) and (4). The individuals in each of these nets tend to **learn** how to transmit successfully (or distort/withhold) messages in the communication process. Any or all of the barriers to communication may be present at any stage.

In net (5) the speed of learning and solution of problems tends to be slow, but because messages can be passed to anyone by anyone, such a group tends to be more flexible and adaptable to change than the other groups and both individual and group morale and satisfaction tend to be quite high.

Feedback is vital, yet in the formal organizational system communication difficulties may arise because:

1. If the net is **long** the speed of transmission within the system will be **slow**.

2. If any member of the net is absent or there is a **blockage**, say for personality reasons, the system may fail to operate effectively/efficiently.

3. It may be difficult to detect message distortions, omissions or errors because of the **hierarchical nature** of the network and the differences associated with backgrounds, social status, responsibilities, reward systems, punishment systems, etc.

It is quite possible (and frequent) for lower members of a hierarchical system to modify or withhold data so that top management's information is incomplete. There are many reasons why such modifications should occur, not the least of which is the ubiquitous problem of individual or group objectives versus the organizational aspirations. Hierarchical communication may thus have several major defects, notably:

1. Only *selective* information may be passed upwards, i.e. information which is good.

2. Those at the bottom may be given *insufficient* information so that they do not know what is important and for whom.

3. A or E may *bypass* intermediaries – with serious effects on B, C and D.

4. The *grapevine* may proliferate, flourish and compensate to some extent.

The communication process in a marketing situation
Consider a firm manufacturing and selling a new furniture polish. It will need *to have* considered:

1. Its corporate **objectives**: long-term and short-term.
2. The product's relationship with other products made by the firm.
3. The competitor's products and sales levels.
4. What *will* make this product saleable?
5. The target group, i.e. the **market segment**.
6. Its **costs** and initial **pricing** strategy.
7. The consumer's **wants** and/or **expectations**.

It will need to *consider:*

1. The **information** which it proposes to give to the consumer.
2. The degree of **persuasion** and **influence** to be exerted.
3. The **medium** to be employed.
4. The **language** to be used.

It will need to assess by **market research** and feedback:

1. Consumer **interpretation** of the message.

2. Consumer **perception** of the product (and the firm).
3. The degree of **noise** which interferes or might interfere with the communication process.

This simplified sequence of events demonstrates the necessity for effective communications, both internally between departments and externally between the firm and its potential and actual market.

PROMOTION

Promotion is part of the firm's total communication function. The promotional aspects of the marketing mix consist of the collection of activities which favourably influence the actual **task** of selling the product to a customer. The major constituent of the promotional mix is **advertising** (indirect demand stimulation) but also important are *personal selling* and detailed *sales promotion* (direct demand stimulation) which includes setting up displays in shops, staging exhibitions and the judicious use of free samples. There are three important ingredients of promotion:

1. Information This is particularly important when a product is new and in industrial marketing.

2. Persuasion In this case it is usually the better promotional mix which tempts the consumer to purchase.

3. Influence The individual and unique properties of a product are stressed, usually because a competitor's similar product is also available and threatening.

ADVERTISING

A common mnemonic has developed which encompasses the advertising strategy, namely **A.I.D.A.**:

A Capture the customer's **attention** and make him **aware** of the product.
I Make an **impact** and stimulate his **interest**.
D Persuade him that he is **deprived** because he does not possess the product and therefore stimulate a **desire** or demand for it.
A **Action**–the actual purchase of the product.

There are difficulties associated with assessing the effectiveness of the promotional expenditure, mainly because of the delayed nature of possible results. In the case of advertising, a distinction is sometimes made between **immediate-impact** and **delayed-impact** advertising. The former category is widely used in industrial marketing, where advertisements in trade journals invite readers to apply for further technical information, and in television advertising, which is particularly useful because different advertising campaigns (and associated costs) may be launched in the various ITV regions, allowing for a certain amount of experimentation. The objectives of an advertising campaign may need:

1. To support an existing brand by stressing its advantages.

2. To attack, directly or indirectly, a competitor and attempt to increase the firm's market share within the total market.

3. To increase total sales by retaining the same market share but within a larger market.

4. To co-operate with producers of jointly-used products to suggest mutual approval.

5. To appeal to a new market segment.

6. To convey an image of the *firm* rather than an actual product.

7. To support a particular marketing *strategy*.

8. To support a decision *to buy after* the purchase has been made.

Most advertising does little more than maintain an existing position, but investigation has shown that this is an essential feature of marketing, for brand loyalty is a very fickle commodity particularly when demand for a product is *elastic*. There are two basic types of advertisement. The first relies on *rational* argument and is relevant, indeed necessary, in industrial marketing and in the launch of new products, such as video cassette recorders. The second type of appeal is to the *emotions* where benefits such as status, safety, personal achievement and sexual success may be conveyed.

The **advertising budget** may be determined:

1. As a *proportion* of anticipated sales revenue – hence the importance of sales forecasting. A firm may also allocate a *percentage* that is based on last year's sales revenue.

2. As *a fixed sum* which may be allocated after taking into consideration the total financial requirements, e.g. in the launch of a new product.

3. As expenditure, allocated as a *cost of each unit* sold.

4. *In comparison* with competitor's expenditure – in effect basing the expenditure on market share.

However, it is necessary to retain a flexible policy so that extra funds might be made available when competitors become particularly aggressive or in order to boost flagging sales.

Media selection will to a great extent depend upon the *coverage* (the number of potential customers reached) required and the *frequency* (the number of times the message is transmitted to the customers). The extent and mix of this media choice is influenced by financial constraints and the market segment at which the product is aimed. In addition, the advertising method chosen must obviously differ with the media selected. The various media available include:

1. Television Regional differentiations; reaches many households but initially expensive; very versatile.

2. Radio, e.g. Radio Luxembourg; other commercial channels.

3. Magazines and journals which are of infinite variety and form, from women's weeklies to highly specific technical journals.

4. Newspapers, including the magazine supplements of some.

5. Posters, including flashing neon lights and advertising on public transport.

6. Direct mail, to potential consumers from up-to-date mailing lists; reaches only the market the advertiser wishes to contact.

7. Outlet advertising, in retail stores.

8. Sports **sponsorship.**

Although enormous sums of money are spent each year on advertising, the expenditure as a percentage of sales is relatively low.
For example:

Commodity	Advertising as a % of sales
Tobacco	4.2
Motion pictures	3.8
Chemicals	3.6
Professional instruments	2.4
Hotels	2.0
Leather products	1.5
Total retail trade	1.4

(Source: *Guide to Consumer Markets (USA)*, 1977)

To devise and launch an advertising campaign a firm may use its own in-house advertising department or commission an *advertising agency* to undertake the whole campaign or use a combination of both. Agencies tend to handle 80–90% of display advertising in the UK.

Factors which influence the promotional mix
There are four basic factors to be considered:

1. The availability of **funds**.
2. The stage of the **Product Life-Cycle (PLC)**.
3. The nature of the **product**.
4. The nature of the **market**.

1. The larger the business the more likely that adequate funding will be available to mount an effective, but not necessarily efficient, advertising campaign, using expensive media such as television and Sunday supplements. In addition, localized advertising may precede a national launch. In launching a new product, *risk capital* rather than loan capital tends to be used as with most ventures. The firm must *budget* wisely for the campaign, consider the associated *opportunity costs* and examine alternative investment strategies.

2. In the development and growth stages of the PLC, the manufacturer's aim is to inform and educate the consumer in order to stimulate demand. As the product moves to the maturity stage, the emphasis tends to change to creating a **brand image** (particularly important in oligopolistic situations) and to counteracting competitors' increased advertising. In order to maintain the sales momentum it may be necessary to offer special promotional offers, including temporary price cuts. This strategy may stimulate sales but it may, of course, reduce total revenue and/or increase associated selling costs. This non-media advertising (or *below-the-line* advertising) is a significant growth area and may include incentives such as free samples, coupon offers, competitions, point-of-sale material, special catalogues, trade-in-deals and free gifts (such as pens and calendars).

3. The nature of the product is closely associated with the nature of the market. Convenience foods, for example, tend to be promoted heavily by point-of-sale displays.

4. The nature of the market considers mainly the geographical segmentation and the differentiation, the degree of concentration of the customers and their various characteristics such as socio-economic groupings and finally the product's appeal to industrial and/or consumer markets.

PERSONAL SELLING

This is the most ubiquitous and frequently utilized ingredient of the promotional mix and often accounts for the largest slice of the firm's operating expenses. It consists of individual personal communication and is therefore more flexible than advertising or sales promotion methods. Its major disadvantage is the high cost associated with remuneration of salaries, commission and travel expenses.

Personal selling has also developed its own mnemonic in order to describe the sequence of events which it entails, namely the 5 Ps:

1. Preparation Salesmen must be familiar with the product, the competition and the market.

2. Prospecting Locating customers and prospective buyers, e.g. through personal announcements such as births, engagements, in local newspapers, etc.

3. Pre-approach Learning something about the customer (or companies) to whom they hope to sell.

4. Presentation Using A.I.D.A.

5. Post-sale support For repeat buying, personal recommendations of the product and follow-up procedures.

The effectiveness of the salesman will be enhanced if he is supported by local and/or national advertising campaigns and sales promotion methods.

PACKAGING

Packaging is a part of the *communications mix* which in turn is an important aspect of the total promotion function. The concept of packaging as a communications medium has acquired considerable influence for, through a distinctive package, many products are readily identifiable particularly on supermarket shelves. Coca-Cola, Daz, SR toothpaste and many more household products have carried their well-known package image for many years. Many products are also identified by a **brand**, which is a name, concept, logo, or abbreviation that is a feature associated with a product, or a range or mix of products, or even a firm such as British Leyland, British Rail, Marks and Spencers (St. Michael) and Kodak. **Branding strategy** is an important aspect of marketing management and company promotional tactics often advertise their distinctive brand rather than a specific product. The firm and its products become synonymous with attributes such as reliability, quality, value, consistency, etc. Brand names are often 'consumer' tested before the final image is selected for eventual use.

The final package choice is influenced by cultural, social and political considerations as well as commercial ones. For example, in many Far East countries, white is the colour of mourning while in Latin American countries the colour purple is associated with death. Some features of the package may serve to stimulate sales – such as a bonus of attractive storage jars to package instant coffee. Clearly, packaging must also fulfil certain functional obligations and in this context it is required to:

1. Provide protection to the product against contamination, spoiling, pilferage, damage and evaporation.

2. Offer convenience in handling, storage and actually dispensing the product, e.g. pressurized canisters for deodorants, hair-lacquers and insect sprays.

The growing importance of self-service stores and the need to display products boldly and attractively has tended to demand even more research and thought into the methods of packaging, of the artwork and design of the label, and of the impact of colour.

Packaging gives the customer an opportunity to become involved *at the moment of decision;* in this sense it is an extremely effective method of communication. Media advertising may *sensitize* the consumer to a particular brand but, at the point of sale, it is the packaging which tips the scales in favour or otherwise of the product.

Chapter 6

The Product (or Services)

Clearly, an organization must have something to offer. This
may be a **service** of some kind or a tangible **product**, but in
order to appeal to existing and potential consumers, and to
attempt to satisfy their needs and wants, products must be
designed to not only fulfil the functional requirement but
also must often possess an idiosyncratic feature which is
deemed attractive/desirable by the consumers. These
idiosyncracies may be of a purely aesthetic kind, or of a
special convenience or of a particular quality. A motor car
may be a motor car but why does a Ford Cortina constantly
head the UK market sales? What was it about the Austin
Metro that caused British Leyland to pin so much hope on
it? What special or different features does it possess? When
attempting to appeal to the mass consumer market,
although competitive products may be similar and produce
the same end result, many factors will influence whether or
not a customer will buy that product, as has already been
discussed in previous chapters.

INDUSTRIAL AND CONSUMER GOODS

On the other hand, the marketing of industrial products is a
much more pragmatic affair. **Industrial goods** are those
which assist the business or organization to discharge its
primary role and carry out its varied and varying duties. The
industrial market is enormous and more than 50% of all
manufactured goods are sold to it. In addition, most of the
raw materials of the primary industries are sold directly to
the industrial markets – raw materials such as timber, coal,
metals and ores, and most of the produce of agriculture and
fishing. However, marketing to industrial consumers is, in
many ways, the same as marketing the finished product to
the final consumer. The market must be analysed and the
product produced, shaped or designed to satisfy the needs of
the industrial market, in which the buyers invariably
attempt to maximize the firm's profit goals. To this end,
minimizing the **variable costs** of the raw materials and
components associated with the manufacture of a finished
product is paramount. Also important are the **capital costs**
associated with the acquisition of fixed assets such as
machinery and plant: industrial purchasers are very sensitive to price differences. It must be remembered, however,
that demand of the industrial market is both derived and
relatively inelastic, even if purchases are usually made less
frequently.

However, very few products will continue to sell forever in
their existing form. Most products will require some
modification or alterations to be made to cater for changing
consumer preferences or in order to cope with the challenge
of competitor's products: if there is profit to be made,
competitors will almost certainly enter the market. A
product may be overtaken not only because of technical

improvement but also by reason of price and/or design as well as functional performance.

Drucker in *The Practice of Management* states that, '...because it is its purpose to create a customer, any business enterprise has two – and only these two – basic functions: marketing and innovation'. To reiterate, the company must invariably be market-oriented, not only in terms of what the customer wants now but what he is likely to want in two, four or six years time – even the customers cannot tell the firm that. Hence, a firm must attempt to anticipate the consumer's requirements and then convince him, eventually, that a new feature is both necessary and desirable. So, a major concern for management must be the content of the **product lines** and this concern should generate the need for a formal **product policy**, the adoption of which has three main advantages:

1. It should provide adequate and relevant **information** for decisions to be made on the product line by those directly involved in the product's manufacture.

2. It provides **guidance** and direction for the activities of the organization towards achieving the major corporate objective and sub-system aspirations.

3. It provides a **framework** against which the product's success can be measured in terms of sales, revenue, promotional effort, competition, etc.

Every company has unique strengths and unfortunate weaknesses and the optimum product policy must attempt to utilize the strong points but, if possible, avoid the weak ones. Some of the strengths upon which a firm might build include:

1. Its financial strength i.e. the investment required to enter a particular market, to control working capital and the stocks of finished goods, work in progress and raw materials, i.e. control of its current assets and the management of liquidity.

2. Sales volume, which partly depends upon the size of the area in which the product will be distributed; are there existing distribution channels or will they have to be created, and paid for? The number of potential customers and the utility and application of the particular product will also be of significance.

3. Channels of distribution including the number of field sales operatives and the number of products they are already handling, the availability of distribution networks and existing or new markets.

4. Competition Where the investment is high the number of competitors will be small, for example, in an oligopolistic market. They may, however, be equally strong. Can the innovating company acquire and hold a sufficient part of the market to ward off any competitive intrusion or threat?

Other salient factors might include:

Research patents Although research and development are expensive, acquiring a patent can be potentially lucrative, particularly if licences can be granted and royalties received, e.g. the production of Coca-Cola in this country.

Raw materials: Backward integration, leading to the acquisition of raw material sources, may give a firm a decided advantage but even more important is the unimpeded supply of raw materials (or components). Ideally, supplies should be from reliable sources, neither too distant nor from sources which are plagued by disruptions such as industrial disputes.

PRODUCT LIFE-CYCLE

It therefore follows that product planning is an essential requirement for any firm, particularly in a multi-product company and/or when the product is not unique. Not only must there be careful planning at all stages of production, but there must also be considered and detailed proposals to ensure a succession of new products, bearing in mind that all products have a life-cycle. Just as an animal is conceived, undergoes a gestation period during which it grows and begins to take shape, is born into infancy, continues to develop, reaches maturity, then declines into old age and finally dies, so too a product travels down a similar path. The major phases are depicted in Figure 25. This concept is known as the **product life-cycle**. Though some authors have defined its limitations, it does aid the management of existing products, and, just as important, may indicate launching tactics associated with successive products.

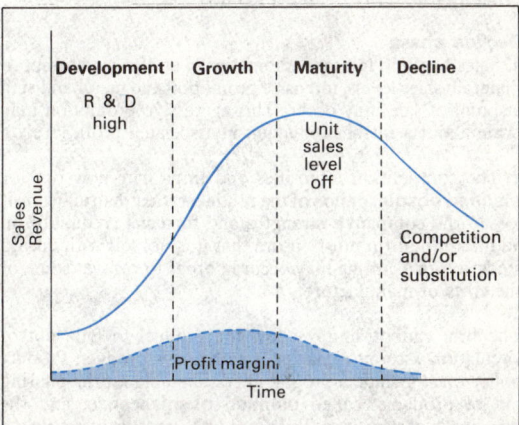

Figure 25. Product life-cycle

The life-cycle phases are marked by:

Development phase
1. Technical innovation and research and development.
2. Initial production difficulties.
3. Determination of channels of distribution.
4. Development and emergence of initial marketing mix and promotional strategy.

During the later stages of this phase, the policy will be firstly to inform potential consumers of the product and secondly to win over consumer acceptance.

Growth phase
1. It now becomes easier to obtain retail outlets, and channels of distribution begin to open up as the market starts to accept the product.

2. Unfortunately, competitors also begin to enter the field but they incur significantly less R & D costs than the innovator who, using intensive promotional campaigns, attempts to establish brand loyalty, particularly if the product lends itself to repeat purchases, e.g. groceries.

Maturation phase
This is either the longest or shortest phase of the life-cycle.

1. As more and more competitors enter the market it reaches saturation point and then there are few, if any, distribution channels to be filled.
2. Sales level off and profits may begin to fall.
3. The innovator trys to modify the original product and second generation products are designed, prepared and tested.
4. Promotion of the firm's name tends to occur rather than promotion of the specific product; emphasis is put on reliability/integrity of the company.

Decline phase
1. Sales begin to fall quite dramatically and, in an attempt to maintain sales levels, intensive promotion and merchandising at point-of-sale may occur. This aggressive promotion may bring about a further reduction in associated profit levels.

2. The competition intensifies and firms may now opt for **planned obsolescence** of the product rather than allowing it to sap the company's strengths and financial credibility. In addition, the firm must ensure that it is not left with unsold stock so price cutting may occur in order to recover some of the costs of manufacture.

The firm cannot simply allow the product to fade out of circulation without replacing it with a new product. Product policy must include a programmed timetable for the phasing out of products, called **planned obsolescence**, and the bringing in of new ones. To this end, the product life-cycle is a useful quantitative guide to management. Some products, of course, appear to have almost indeterminate life-cycles, e.g.

Colman's mustard, while others are very transitory, e.g. ladies' fashions and skateboards. So a product phasing strategy is particularly important in multi-product companies where many of the products may be comparatively short lived.

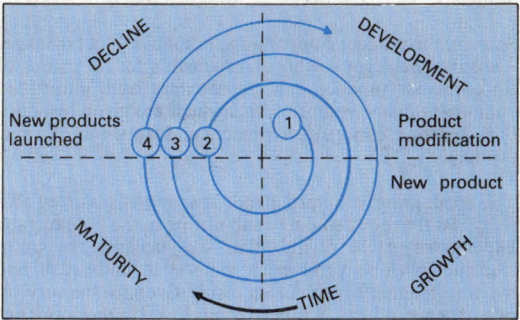

Figure 26. Launch strategy

No sooner is one product launched, than another must be in the design stage to replace it. This concept is illustrated in Figure 26. Before a product is withdrawn from the market, the next product must be well into its growth phase.

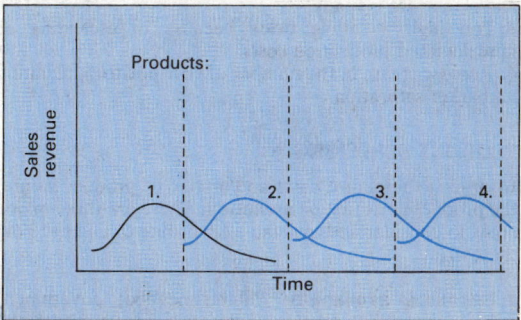

Figure 27. Successive product launches

Only by ensuring *successive* products which are acceptable to the final user – whether industrial or consumer – will the firm ensure its own survival. No product vacuum must ever occur. Competition and the introduction of alternatives or substitutes are the major factors which influence the length of the product life-cycle. Yet, another important factor is the associated pricing policy. In essence, product policy can be compared with the activities and aspirations of a keen gardener who seeks to have interesting, if not flowering, exhibits all the year round rather than a mass of blooms in the spring and summer and a dull, lifeless garden for the remainder of the year. In the same way that new products must be planned and developed long before an earlier product reaches its decline phase, so too product **extension**

strategies must be formulated early, probably before the original product is launched. The basic ideas associated with extending the life-span of a particular product, and thereby retaining a market share, include the promotion of the product's more *varied usage* and deliberately *modifying the product* to meet the needs of new customers.

Some multi-product companies appoint a product manager – a *brand* manager – who is responsible for all phases of his particular product; other companies have introduced *multi-disciplinary* venture teams which are given responsibility for the creation, development and launching of a new product.

This small group of interdependent specialists is often able to bypass the requirement of submitting to the bureaucratic imperatives of the organization and, because the group identifies with its product, a motivated, innovative and dynamic team effort can often result. Even so, the survival rate of new products is still extremely low. If a product is not eliminated during a viability investigation within the firm, it may still **fail**, when launched, for the following reasons:

1. Inadequate marketing effort and poorly trained/motivated marketing/sales personnel.
2. Premature entry into the market before the product and/or market is ready.
3. Too high a selling **price** because of escalating or miscalculated production costs.
4. Rapid increase in the number of **competitors**, resulting in market saturation.

PRODUCT SCREENING

In order to minimize costs and/or risk of product failure, the product must first be **screened**. There are three major areas to consider and evaluate. According to Giles (1974) these are:

1. Resource availability Capital needed; government policy, e.g. special development areas; opportunity costs; labour availability and training costs; availability of raw materials; effect on resources necessary for the manufacture of other products; can existing resources be utilized, e.g. distribution networks.

2. Demand factors Market segmentation; seasonal or stable sales; promotional elasticity; extension possibilities.

3. The Competition Are product substitutes available?; consider the use of Interfirm Comparisons (B.I.M.) in assessing performance, costs, etc.; patent/copyright possibilities; potential number of competitors and their comparative strengths and weaknesses.

A schematic outline of product planning and associated activities is shown in Figure 28.

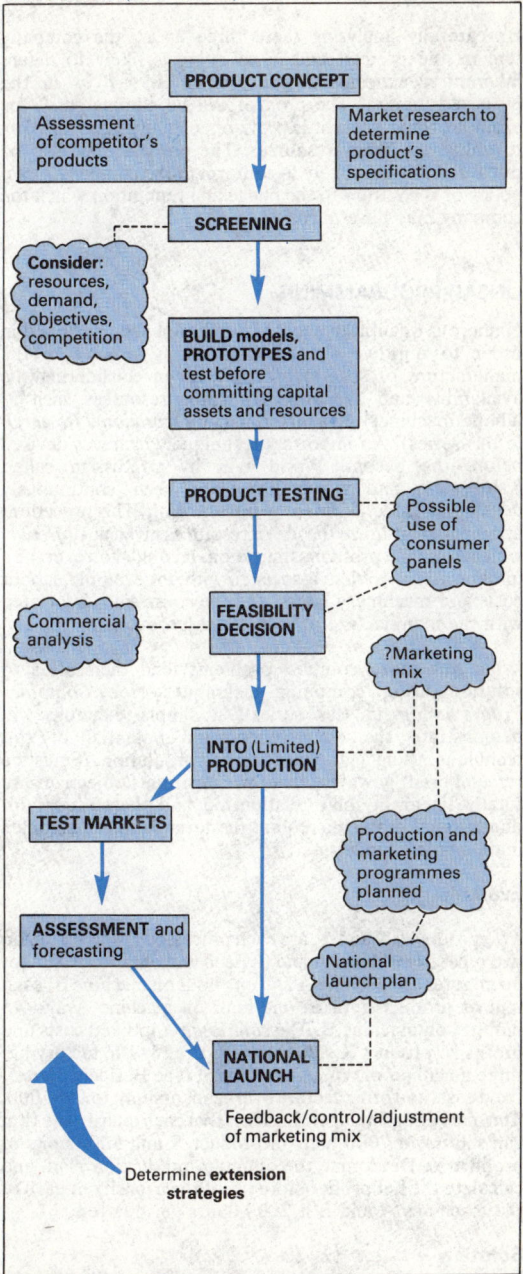

PRODUCT CONCEPT

Assessment of competitor's products

Market research to determine product's specifications

SCREENING

Consider: resources, demand, objectives, competition

BUILD models, PROTOTYPES and test before committing capital assets and resources

PRODUCT TESTING

Possible use of consumer panels

FEASIBILITY DECISION

Commercial analysis

?Marketing mix

INTO (Limited) **PRODUCTION**

TEST MARKETS

Production and marketing programmes planned

ASSESSMENT and forecasting

National launch plan

NATIONAL LAUNCH

Feedback/control/adjustment of marketing mix

Determine **extension strategies**

Figure 28. Product planning

By carefully analysing these three areas, the company screens the product and in so doing is likely to detect inherent weaknesses in the product *as well as* in the proposed market. The product will be eliminated if, for example, there is too little profit opportunity or if it is likely to utilize too many resources. The product may also be discarded if it is unlikely to conform to the company's own policy or is contrary to the image and reputation which the company may have nurtured.

LINEAR PROGRAMMING

Numerous quantitative techniques have been developed in order to improve the decision-making process in the manufacture of several products, when considering the availability and allocation of scarce resources such as labour, machinery, raw materials (see *Operational Research* in this series). An important technique which was devised before the Second World War by a Russian called Kantrovich, and which has since been continuously developed, is that of **linear programming**. This procedure attempts to optimize the use of resources given an *objective,* which is usually profit maximization. It could, however, be a minimization problem associated with, for example, labour costs and machinery hours, and the *constraints* associated with the manufacture of each of the products.

While the more complex problems lend themselves to solution using computer techniques (see *Computer Programming* in this series), a simple example will demonstrate the effectiveness and potential of this technique, using a graphical method of solution. It must be remembered, however, that few constraints/objectives are totally linear in their relationship and therefore multi-dimensional problems require the formulation of complex mathematical models.

Example

Two products, X and Y, are each processed in succession on two types of machine, A and B. Each unit of product X takes 30 minutes on machine A and one hour on machine B; each unit of product Y takes one hour on machine A and 45 minutes on machine B. The *contribution* to fixed costs and profits is: product X, £20; product Y, £25. The factory has three machines of type A and four of type B. Each quarter, fixed costs and other factory overheads amount to £150 000. The marketing manager considers that each quarter the firm can sell up to 7000 units of product X and 5000 units of product Y. Determine the optimum production plan, and calculate the net profit before tax, if the capacity of each of the machines A and B is 2000 hours per quarter.

Solution

1. Determine the objective, i.e. maximize 20X + 25Y.

2. Determine the constraints.

Product	Machine A	Machine B
X	0.5	1
Y	1	0.75
Capacity (hours)	6 000	8 000

Therefore $0.5X + 1Y \leqslant 6000$
$1X + 0.75Y \leqslant 8000$
also $X \leqslant 7000$
$Y \leqslant 5000$

Transfer these constraints to a graph, as shown in Figure 29.

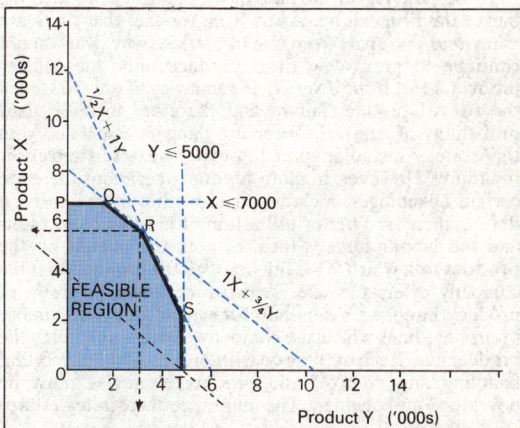

Figure 29. Linear programming — graphical solution

The output can lie anywhere in the region bounded by the heavy black line; this is known as the **feasible area**. Neither product can be produced outside of this area because of the constraints associated with each product.

The optimum solution is determined by superimposing the contribution relationship between the two products, i.e. the contribution of product X is £20 and that of product Y is £25 – the objective function.

The relationship is linear. If a contribution of, say, £10 000 is assumed, then X can be 500 **or** Y can be 400. Plot these two points on the graph and join them. The resulting line is known as the **trial profit line**. The optimum solution will be found on a profit line drawn *parallel* to the trial profit line but as far away from the origin as possible. This solution will be at one of the corners or vertices of the feasible area.

So, referring to Figure 29, the optimum solution is to be found at point R:

About 5800 of product X (at £20 each) = 116 000
About 3200 units of product Y (£25 each) =   80 000
                                             _____
                              Contribution   £196 000

At any other point within the feasible area the contribution is less. Now, if the fixed costs are £150 000 per quarter, net profit before tax would be £46 000 per quarter.

Other mathematical techniques used in product planning, and discussed fully in other books in this series, include model building, Bayesian statistics, decision trees and probability, queuing problems and critical path analysis.

In theory, the bigger the market for the firm's product, the bigger the firm can be. Apart from the fact that there are many reasons, apart from size of market, why firms do not continue to grow, few firms produce only one solitary product. Most firms diversify in some way, if only to spread the risk of product failure and therefore increase their probability of survival. There are dangers associated with this strategy, including spreading expertise, assets and effort too thinly. However, in multi-product operations there are certain advantages, including a reduction in the costs of development and better utilization of existing fixed assets and the labour force. Much, of course, depends on the **product mix** which is the full list of all the products that the company offers for sale. A **product line** is a group of products intended, essentially, for similar uses. The number of product lines which the company carries constitutes the product mix. Each of these constituents requires purposeful handling and control, and product strategies must be developed and planned. The major product strategies are:

1. Planned obsolescence.
2. Increasing the number of product lines or depth (size, colours) of a product line.
3. Pruning the product mix (importance of the product life-cycle) by eliminating a product line.
4. Modifying the package or the design of an existing product.

Essentially, when management selects and develops a product it is also selecting the kind of business the firm is *going* to be in tomorrow. The product launches the product-sales-revenue-profit-survival cycle. The implications inherent in this cycle should be sufficient to ensure sensitive and responsive product planning and policy formation.

Chapter 7

Pricing

Companies, invariably, are anxious to satisfy their shareholders by distributing a satisfactory, i.e. acceptable, dividend, and therefore the firm must earn **normal profit**, which is the amount just necessary to persuade the investors to keep their capital invested in the firm. Although it may seem paradoxical, normal profit is a vital part of the firm's costs: above this level, it is called **supernormal profit** which is not included in costs. Normal profit is always included in costs and is essential to maintain a minimum investment level.

A company must sell in a market in order to earn revenue from which profit may ultimately be deducted, but a market is not simply or necessarily a place where a product may be exhibited and inspected. It refers to the group of conditions which arise when seller and buyer are brought into contact. In economic terms, there are two types of market:

1. Perfect (or pure competition) markets.
2. Imperfect markets.

The perfect market is relatively rare and almost all commercial organizations operate in an imperfect market.

PERFECT AND IMPERFECT MARKETS

Perfect markets
There is a general tendency for only one price to prevail in the market at any one time, subject to differences due to costs of transport and customs duties (if any). Though few commodities are suitable for dealings in a perfect market, the market for stocks and shares – the Stock Exchange – is often quoted as being near perfect.

In a perfect market:

1. There are many *producers* and *buyers;* one firm or consumer cannot affect price.
2. Products are *homogeneous*.
3. There is unrestricted entry.
4. *Price uniformity* may lead to pure oligopoly because of economies of scale.
5. Cartels may form.

In such a market the buyer is indifferent from whom he buys and the seller indifferent to whom he sells.

Imperfect markets
Few markets are perfect; the majority are imperfect if only because information is imperfect, including price changes. Imperfect markets are, however, a feature of sophisticated, mixed economies.

In an imperfect market:

1. The prices are *not uniform;* buyers do not always seek the cheapest source of supply.
2. A firm may change its price(s) and affect other firms by doing so.
3. Freedom of entry is restricted.
4. Differentiated products may lead to differentiated oligopolies.
5. Price wars may occur but are usually destructive, e.g. petrol.
6. There is often much brand advertising and product and packaging innovation, e.g. motor cars, cigarettes, soaps and detergents.

In an imperfect market, then, what is the price which a company may obtain for its product or services? Clearly, price must be related to **value**, a term which expresses the relationship between two commodities, i.e. the amount of one commodity that must be given in exchange for another. Although bartering still takes place, e.g. trading-in a used car, the normal medium of exchange which is used is that of money. However, an essential feature of value is that of **scarcity**. It follows that the larger the supply of a product relative to the demand, the less is its value, and the smaller the supply, the greater is its value. So, a product (or service) has value if it satisfies three characteristics:

1. Utility, i.e. it is capable of satisfying a want.
2. Scarcity.
3. If it can be transferred from seller to buyer.

In economic terms, it is these three characteristics and their relationships which will influence the product's ultimate price. So *price* is simply value expressed in terms of money.

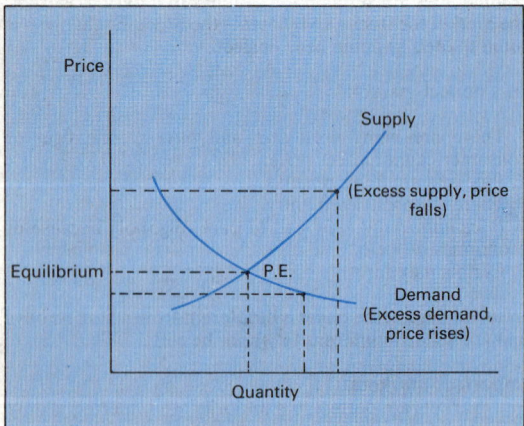

Figure 30. Price equilibrium

The interaction of supply and demand in the market will determine price. Price tends towards that level which equates supply with demand, i.e. **price equilibrium**, as shown in Figure 30.

With excess *supply,* stocks accumulate and prices fall. With excess *demand* there are insufficient stocks and prices rise. When supply and demand are in equilibrium there is little price change, but demand (and not supply) tends to be the dominant influence in the determination of market price, which is always a temporary price.

DETERMINING THE MARKET PRICE

There are six major determinants of the final market price:

1. Consumer demand which is influenced by the reputation of the company, promotional elasticity and the demand for other products.

2. Competitors and their share of the market, their promotional campaign and costs incurred (again, the use of Interfirm Comparisons will give some indication) and their reputation.

3. Time-scale Pricing as a short-term measure or tactic, e.g. penetration pricing, or as a long-term strategy, e.g. satisfactory rate of return method.

4. Environmental, e.g. the effects of government legislation, such as prices and incomes policies and macroeconomic policies as measures to control inflation, availability of subsidies and grants, EEC policies and social costs such as those of pollution.

5. Other parts of the marketing mix and, particularly, the firm's hierarchy of **objectives**.

6. Costs which require a more detailed examination.

In order to arrive at an economically acceptable price, an analysis of the associated costs incurred in the production and marketing of a product must be determined. Several methods are in use. The simplest is the cost-plus approach.

Cost-plus approach This is based on the selling price for a unit of a particular product being equal to the unit's total cost plus an arbitrary amount or percentage added to produce a satisfactory profit. Unfortunately, this method, while commonly used, ignores the fact that there are different *types* of costs and that not all of them act alike as output increases or decreases. In addition, this method tends to ignore market forces. For example, revenue may be based on the sale of all units yet demand may be inadequate and some units remain unsold; unit costs remain the same but overheads must be paid, therefore profit per unit falls significantly.

Example
A builder builds 20 houses; the labour and materials (direct costs) cost him £200000; other indirect overheads (such as administration, interest payments, salaries and depreciation on fixed assets) total a further £100000. He plans a 20% return on costs and therefore decides to sell each house for £18000. Unfortunately, he can sell only 15 of the houses. Profit per house is now much less because the indirect overheads must now be charged to the 15 houses rather than being spread over 20 houses.

	£		£
Unit cost = 10000 × 20	= 200000	Cost of 15 houses	= 150000
Indirect overheads	= 100000	Indirect overheads	= 100000
			250000
20% mark up	= 60000		
To be received	= 360000	Revenue: 15 × 18000	= 270000
		Actual loss	= (30000)

(The builder does, of course, now have five completed houses in stock.) Those who advocate cost-plus pricing do so mainly because of its *simplicity* and *ease of determination*. More sophisticated and accurate costing procedures are available and include **marginal (or variable) costing**.

A **marginal cost** is the addition to the total cost resulting from a *one unit increase in output,* i.e. a cost that would be avoided if the unit was not produced.
Fixed costs are those costs which remain the same in the short term (in the long term *all* costs change) until a ceiling in output is reached, and more capital must be injected in order to further increase output. Examples of fixed costs are rent, rates, depreciation, salaries and interest payments.
Variable costs are those *direct* costs associated with producing each unit of output, notably wages, materials and energy costs. Certain other costs are known as **semi-variable**, e.g. telephone – rental-fixed, usage-variable.
Consider the following table:

Output (units)	Total fixed cost	Total variable cost	Total cost	Marginal cost	Average cost
0	200				
1	200	40	240	140	140
2	200	70	270	30	135
3	200	88	288	18*	96
4	200	108	308	20	77
5	200	135	335	27	67
6	200	172	372	37	62
7	200	220	420	48	60*
8	200	280	480	60	60*
9	200	358	558	78	62
10	200	460	660	102	66

It is now possible to pinpoint which additional unit can be produced most cheaply. It is *not* the same as the lowest average cost.

It follows that **marginal revenue (MR)** is the revenue which the firm obtains from the *sale* of one more unit. Consider the following diagram, Figure 31.

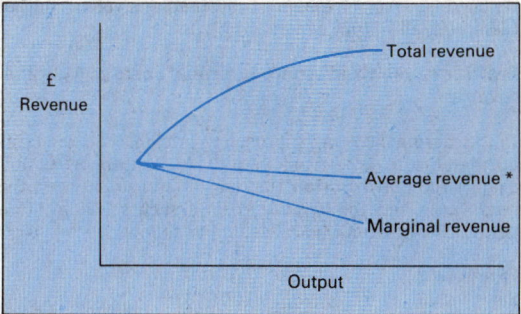

Figure 31. Revenue/output relationship

$$*\text{Average revenue (AR)} = \frac{\text{Total revenue}}{\text{No. of units sold}}$$

In Figure 31, total revenue is *not* rising steadily, i.e. the firm is *not* getting the same amount for each additional unit sold (MR); MR must be falling, therefore AR is falling as the marginal revenue pulls it down. The firm can only sell more by reducing the price (or in the short term increasing costs, e.g. on advertising and/or sales promotion).

Figure 32 shows what happens when the concepts of marginal costs and marginal revenues are combined.

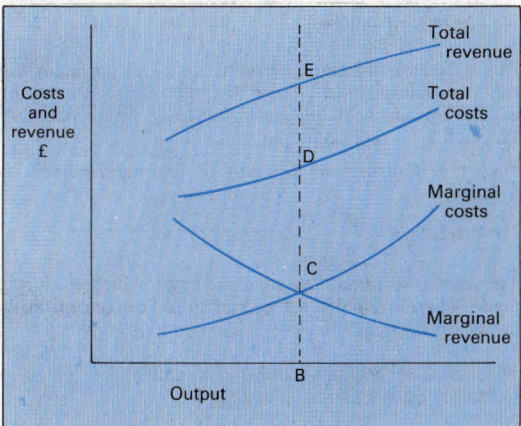

Figure 32. Marginal revenue/marginal costs

AB is the level of output where MC = MR. Before point C, MC is lower than MR, so production continues until AB is reached. After point C, the MC is higher than MR so production is restricted to AB.

The vertical distance between total revenue and total costs is profit. At AB this is DE; before or after AB, DE is reduced so AB is the most profitable level of output (assuming all output can be sold!).

Profit is maximized where marginal costs = Marginal revenue.

In the marginal costing approach to pricing, the fixed costs attributable to a relevant period are written off in full against the **contribution** (i.e. the difference between the *sales value* and the *variable cost* of such sales) for that period. Profit would be calculated as follows:

Example 1

Sales value	£100 000
Variable cost of sales	(40 000)
Contribution	60 000
Fixed costs	(30 000)
Profit before tax	30 000

Example 2

Swan Joinery Ltd can produce either product X or product Y with existing facilities. The following information relates to each unit produced and sold:

	Product X	Product Y
Selling price	£40	£34
Variable cost	28	30
Apparent contribution	12	4

But in the case of Swan Joinery there is a limiting factor – in this case labour hours; there are only 800 labour hours available each week. Product X takes 8 hours per unit. Product Y takes 2 hours per unit.

Now the contribution per unit of limiting factor is as follows:

For product X $= \dfrac{12}{8} = £1.50$; for product Y $= \dfrac{4}{2} = £2.00$.

The fixed costs remain the same no matter which product is made. Therefore profit will be maximized by concentrating on product Y, e.g.

Product X   800 hours ÷ 8 = 100 units
Contribution = £12 × 100 = <u>£1200</u>

Product Y   800 hours ÷ 2 = 400 units
Contribution = £4 × 400 = <u>£1600</u>

Marginal costing separates contribution to fixed costs and to profits and may be used when decisions have to be made regarding the most profitable product to manufacture. The greatest profit will be earned by maximizing the contribution per unit of **limiting factor** (such as labour, raw materials or machine capacity). It is essential, however, that no costs are omitted, although it is often difficult to separate fixed costs and variable costs.

Using this approach, it is apparent that a product must not be regarded as weak simply because it does not contribute to profits; it may contribute significantly to fixed costs. It might therefore be imprudent to discontinue that product, for the contribution from remaining products would have to be reallocated to cover the extra fixed costs and the total profit would effectively be reduced. The following example demonstrates this point.

Example
Some costs, such as cleaning, heating and security, are difficult to apportion to a specific department and these indirect overheads may be *allocated* to departments using some arbitrary measure such as floor area, number of personnel employed or number of radiators in the department.
Consider the Morris Departmental Store (floor area in square feet).

Total floor area	600 000
Men's fashions	50 000
Ladies' fashions	100 000
Haberdashery	50 000
Gardening and DIY	100 000
Toys	50 000
Furniture	100 000
Cafe	50 000

Total indirect overheads for one year amount to £250 000.

Sales and variable costs of each sales department are as follows:

	Men's	Ladies'	Haber.	DIY	Toys	Furnit.	Cafe
Sales	250 000	400 000	200 000	300 000	150 000	200 000	50 000
V.C.	200 000	250 000	150 000	150 000	125 000	120 000	30 000
Contr.	50 000	150 000	50 000	150 000	25 000	80 000	20 000
Allocated indirect overheads*	25 000	50 000	25 000	50 000	25 000	50 000	25 000
Profit	25 000	100 000	25 000	100 000	–	30 000	(5 000)

*(per square area)

Although the cafe appears to be showing a net loss, it is contributing £20 000 towards the total indirect overheads. If the cafe did not exist the £25 000 apportioned to it would still need to be paid by the other departments. (The cafe area might, of course, be reallocated to a profitable department.) In addition, of course, it is a complementary service to the other departments which would not do as well if the cafe was closed. The costs of administration must be paid for by the selling departments, i.e. 500 000 sq. ft. For example, men's fashions occupies one tenth of this area, therefore £250 000 ÷ 10 = £25 000 in allocated indirect overheads.

The importance of fixed and variable costs is also demonstrated in the construction of break-even charts which are another tool of price determination.

BREAK-EVEN ANALYSIS (BEA)

This indicates approximate profit or loss at different *levels of activity*. The distance between the level of activity at which the firm is operating and the break-even point is known as the **margin of safety**.

$$\text{Break-even point (BEP)} = \frac{\text{Fixed costs (total)}}{\text{Unit selling price} - \text{Unit variable cost}}$$

e.g. FC = 50 000; Unit SP = £8; Unit VC = £5

$$\text{BEP} = \frac{50\,000}{8-5} = \frac{50\,000}{3} = \underline{16\,667} \text{ units}$$

which at £8 each = £133 336 of revenue.

This may also be demonstrated graphically, as shown in Figure 33.

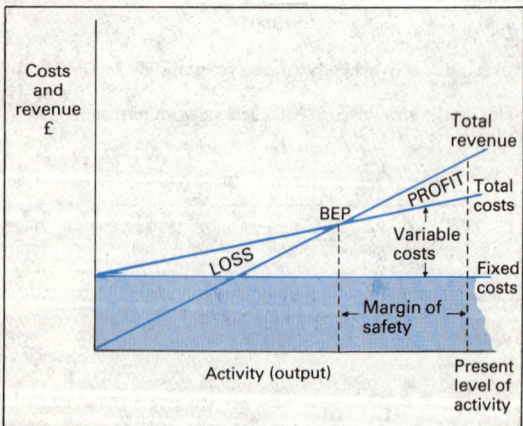

Figure 33. Break-even analysis

The break-even chart determines at what level of output (assuming the output is sold) the revenue will equal the cost, assuming *neither costs nor selling price change,* which is an unreasonable assumption. It must be remembered that total fixed costs will remain constant only over a *short* period of time. Another assumption is that variable costs per unit will also remain constant. This too is most unlikely for the major variable costs – labour and raw materials – will certainly change, even without inflationary economic conditions. In addition, as the volume of output increases it may be possible to achieve **economies of scale** as a result of which costs per unit may actually fall. If the capacity of the firm can be increased, a lower cost per unit may be achieved because:

1. Larger machines and equipment cost proportionately less to buy and maintain, e.g. a six-tonne lorry does not need two drivers: two 3-tonne lorries do.

2. There is increasing scope for the **division of labour** and specialized machinery.

3. Administrative economies.

4. It may be possible to **bulk buy** raw materials so earning valuable discounts.

5. Marketing economies may be achieved, particularly as regards automated packaging and utilizing existing outlets.

Also, proportionately less fixed costs are spread over a greater number of units produced.

The break-even chart does presume that the company can sell its output at any price, which is quite unrealistic. However, by superimposing *a demand curve* and calculating total revenue over a *range* of prices, the optimum price can be determined.

Profit/volume charts
Another way of showing the cost/revenue information graphically is by use of a profit/volume chart, as shown in Figure 34. Sales are shown on the horizontal axis; the loss when activity is nil is equal to the fixed costs; the profit line cuts the sales axis at the break-even point.

Example
J.R. Fords Ltd manufactures three products, A, B and C. Last month's figures are as follows:

Product	A	B	C	Total
Sales	40000	50000	60000	150000
Variable costs	20000	30000	50000	100000
Contribution	20000	20000	10000	50000
Fixed costs				35000
Profit before tax				15000

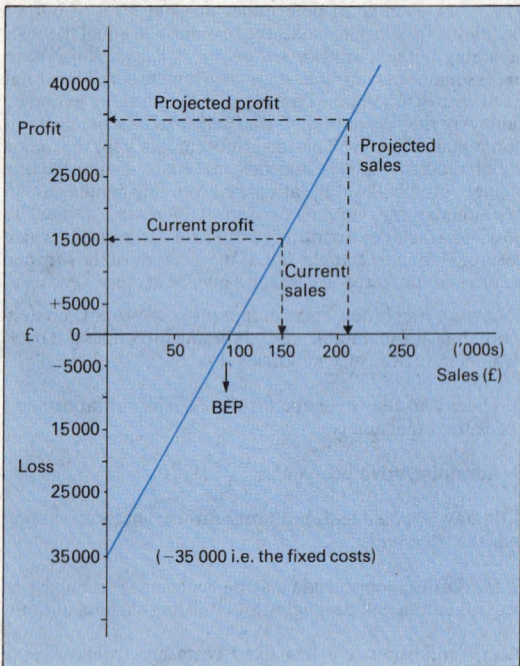

Figure 34. Profit/volume chart

The profit/volume ratio (P/V) = $\dfrac{\text{Contribution}}{\text{Sales}}$

and indicates the slope of the line on the P/V chart.

The P/V ratio for J.R. Fords Ltd is $\dfrac{50\,000}{150\,000}$ = one third.

The P/V ratio allows for the calculation of the contribution for any level of sales. Suppose Fords could achieve sales of £210 000; the contribution would be one third of £210 000 = £70 000. Providing fixed costs remain the same at £35 000, profit would now be £35 000 per month.

While these pricing techniques are useful, the final price is still often *market inspired,* i.e. the price is set at the market level which has already been established by competitors and which management knows, from experience, will be accepted by the consumer.

The basic pricing strategies include:

1. Competitive pricing Pricing at the 'going-rate' which rests on several assumptions, particularly that the product is as acceptable and as good as that of the competition. However, the more *homogeneous* products are, the more prices must change *simultaneously*. It must be remembered that the firm's cost base may also be very different from that of the competition.

2. Market penetration Setting a below competition price in order to capture a share of the market – even to the point of sustaining a loss – in the hope that the price may be raised subsequently after some brand loyalty has been obtained. However, this strategy is potentially dangerous in inflationary conditions.

3. Skimming Particularly useful when launching a unique product for which the initial price may often be very high – sometimes going up-market to the higher SEGs – then leaving the market when competition becomes threatening or reducing the price significantly when consumer resistance becomes apparent.

4. Variable pricing Diurnal pricing, e.g. telephone charges, or seasonal pricing, e.g. holidays and hotels.

To summarize, the primary pricing objectives are:

1. To obtain a satisfactory return (i.e. a **target return**) on investment or sales.
2. To meet and counter **competition**.
3. To establish a **quantified target share** of the market.
4. To optimize profits and ensure **corporate survival**.

Despite the contents of this chapter, it must be emphasized that pricing theory, particularly as presented in a microeconomic analysis of the firm, has been criticized on two main counts:

1. That firms do not seek to maximize profits but resort to satisficing, and

2. That detailed information related to costs, competition and demand is simply not available to the firm – hence the importance of **market pricing** and/or satisfactory rate of return.

Chapter 8

The Place

PHYSICAL DISTRIBUTION MANAGEMENT

So far, the following aspects have been introduced and examined:

1. The enterprise as a **total system** and the role of marketing as a **sub-system**.

2. The search for and analysis of **information** relevant to the marketing process in particular and the vitality and responsiveness of the company as a whole.

3. The **behavioural aspects** of consumer purchasing, motivation and **market segmentation**.

4. The definition of **corporate objectives** and the associated planning and control measures through which the goals might be achieved.

5. The nature and effects of intra-organizational and external **communications, promotion** and **packaging** as part of the communications mix.

6. The product and associated **corporate policy**; the product life-cycle, effects at various phases and how the life-cycle might be extended.

7. Pricing and the use of accurate and realistic costing procedures, particularly the assessment of **contribution** to fixed costs and profit and pricing strategies.

So the company knows what it wants to achieve; it has a product to market and knows, initially, the price it proposes to ask for that product and has decided how it is going to promote it and to which market segment it intends to appeal. Now it must get the product to the industrial user or final consumer, **i.e. the place**, using an effective and efficient distribution system. The centre for **Physical Distribution Management (PDM)** was established in 1970. This organization defines physical distribution management as:

> . . .the broad range of activities, within a company, concerned with the efficient movement of goods and materials both *inwards* to the point of manufacture and *outwards* from the production line to the customer. . .

In order to achieve this, PDM embraces far more than simply the physical movement of goods, i.e. transportation; it is also responsible for effective warehousing and stock control systems and order systems, the detailed planning of depot locations, delivery schedules, drop sizes, etc. Physical distribution can be a substantial element in the total process of satisfying the customer, particularly in regard to product availability and **lead time** and the direct financial value of a prompt service.

Aspects of stock and inventory control are presented in the accompanying book *Production* in this series. In this Chapter, attention will be concentrated on **channels of distribution** and the associated **middlemen**.

A channel of distribution is the route taken by the *title* to the goods as they move from producer to the final customer or industrial user. This is not necessarily the same as the channel used for the physical movement of those goods. A **middleman** consists of an independent business concern which gives a service connected with the purchase or sale of the goods between producer and ultimate consumer or industrial user. Often, a middleman owns the goods, i.e. he takes the title, or he may negotiate transfer of the title, e.g. an estate agent. **Merchant** middlemen actually take ownership title to the goods, e.g. wholesalers and retailers; **agent** middlemen negotiate transfer of the title but never own the goods, e.g. stock brokers and mail-order agents.

Many manufacturers have tended to lose much of the personal relationship with customers as channels of distribution have become more sophisticated and complex. In agriculture, the pattern of selling is particularly complex because there are many farmers and widespread demand for the product, much of which is perishable in the short term and which requires minimum handling. To facilitate distribution and standardize quality and prices, **Marketing Boards** have been established. The primary aims of these Boards are to regulate the marketing and to encourage efficient production. In addition, they assume collective responsibility for promotion of the product and research into new forms or new uses, e.g. the Potato Marketing Board has a continuing programme of research into the development of disease resistant varieties and those from which an increased yield can be achieved.

(The Agricultural Marketing Act which was passed in 1931 gave powers to not less than two thirds of the producers of an agricultural product to prepare a marketing scheme.)

In manufacturing industries, supplies may be adjusted more easily to meet the exigencies of demand and the products can be standardized and stored before distribution, although there are costs associated with storage such as warehousing charges, e.g. inventory control, wages, air-conditioning, lighting, opportunity costs, etc.

Therefore the major factors which influence the channel of trading and distribution include:

1. The *nature of the product,* e.g. its perishability and value.
2. The *size* and *output* of producing units.
3. The *geographical dispersion* of such units and depot locations.

4. The *size of the market,* its location and concentration.
5. The *nature of demand,* whether it is steady or seasonal, consumer or industrial.
6. The amount and quality of *advice* and after-sales service which may be required.
7. The degree and extent of *promotion* which is considered necessary.

In essence, the essential criteria to be considered are: **market coverage, cost** and **channel control**.

THE DISTRIBUTION CHAIN

In industrial marketing there is a strong tradition of direct sale or supply from manufacturers to the industrial consumer but in the distribution of consumer goods the supplier may utilize the services of wholesalers and/or retailers. Whichever channel is used depends significantly on the consumer's purchasing habits and it is these which ultimately influence the method of distribution. It may be necessary, or at the least desirable, to have a number of channels available in order to retain flexibility and maintain adequate supply and sales.

The channels of distribution are shown in Figure 35.

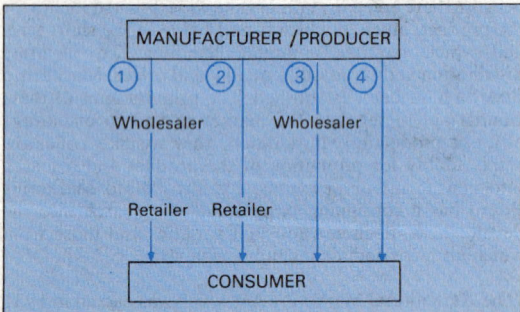

Figure 35. The distribution chain

Distribution methods (3) and (4) have been encouraged by modern and improved methods of communication and transport, and better methods of packaging, market research and advertising.

The wholesaler
The wholesaler remains an important link in the commercial network even though there is an increasing propensity for manufacturers to supply the final customer directly, in which case the manufacturer must assume the role and functions of the wholesaler (i.e. develop a *vertical* marketing system). A wholesaler must attempt to reconcile supply and demand. In doing so he helps to relieve the manufacturer of this task.

The principle services which the traditional **wholesaler** offers to **retailers/customers** are as follows:

1. He offers a variety of **choice** from many manufacturers, depending upon the exclusivity of the distribution network.

2. He **breaks bulk** and may be prepared to release the product in smaller batches than many manufacturers are prepared to do, because of the associated costs, order processing and stock control procedures which would be additional to the manufacturing role.

3. He is often situated **locally** which facilitates easier communication between him and the retailers/consumers. In addition, many wholesalers provide a quick and reliable **delivery service**.

4. Because he may be dealing with several manufacturers, he is able to keep abreast of competitive product innovation and development and to advise his customers accordingly. In this context, he is an important link in the marketing **communication mix**.

5. He may **grade, pre-pack** and **even price** the products so that they are ready for immediate retail sale and he may also offer help and advice with point-of-sale promotion and merchandising of the products.

The wholesaler also gives valuable service to the **manufacturer** in that:

1. He helps to expand and **create markets**, perhaps with the tangible assistance of the manufacturer who may offer trade discounts and emphasize promotional offers.

2. He is able to make the manufacturers aware of changing **consumer preferences** and the nature of demand for other products and associated market trends.

3. To some extent he is able to **stabilize prices** by varying supplies and by stock-holding (although at a cost).

4. He **relieves** the manufacturer of some **risk** by taking title to the goods and therefore losses owing to factors such as spoilage, pilfering or fashion obsolescence are borne by him.

However, despite the advantages which they offer, wholesalers tend to be caught between large-scale direct-buying retailers such as Sainsburys and Marks and Spencer on the one hand and large-scale direct selling manufacturers on the other hand. There are many occasions when a wholesaler, acting as a middleman, is either not required or not appropriate, as when:

1. The manufacturer appoints sole agents, e.g. exclusive rights *(franchise)* to sell British Leyland cars in a particular town.

2. The manufacturer can supply retailers directly such as the large supermarket chains, which either have strategically placed depot warehouses or are sufficiently large to carry considerable stocks themselves, e.g. hypermarkets like Asda. Similarly, when there are many smaller local retailers geographically concentrated, it may be cheaper and easier for the manufacturer to supply these retailers directly either by using his own transport – particularly when handling must be minimized, e.g. frozen foods and crockery – or by contracting out the distribution to a transport organization such as National Carriers.

3. The manufacturer/producer owns his own retail outlets, e.g. farm shops, wool mill shops.

4. Products are large or very expensive or sales relatively slow, e.g. microcomputers, furniture. Many multiple chain stores specialize in the retailing of a particular kind of product and the manufacturer is able to provide bulk supply either to individual stores or to depot locations.

5. The product is either custom-made or requires complex mechanical/electrical installation and after-sales service or when the manufacturer wants closer market contact.

Bonded warehouses
Bonded warehouses are used to store products, usually imported (whisky and cigarettes being the exceptions), which are located at docks and airports. These warehouses are established and provided by importers or companies to store those goods 'in bond', i.e. pending the payment of the appropriate customs and/or excise duty. The owner of the goods is allowed to inspect the goods and may even work on them, e.g. for packaging or blending purposes, but the goods cannot be released until the duty has been paid or a *guarantee* that it will be paid is given by the owner.

While the traditional role of some wholesalers has declined over the past 30 years or so, many have responded by establishing an exclusive service to voluntary chain stores such as Mace, Spar and Vivo. These retail outlets – small independent grocers – collectively enjoy the discounts and economies of scale which they could not as individuals achieve. In addition, belonging to the organization brings additional benefits associated with promotion, advertising and the establishment of individual businesses. Similarly, cash'n carry stores, such as Robert Daniels Ltd, have been established to serve *bone fide* retailers, hoteliers and caterers; shopping for personal needs by individual customers is not allowed, for such a practice would threaten the livelihood of individual retailers.

RETAILING
Retailing includes all activities related directly to the sale of goods or services to the **final consumer** for his personal use. The major retail outlets in the UK are:

1. Independent traders.
2. Multiple shops.
3. Voluntary chain stores.
4. Departmental stores.
5. Supermarkets and hypermarkets.
6. Mail-order retailing.
7. Others, including market stalls, factory shops, farm shops, etc.

A brief description of some types of retail outlets is given below.

1. Department stores

The development of department stores in the UK began in about 1860, but the concept of a single large store with many departments originated in Paris where the bon marché was established in 1852. There are three basic reasons for the growth of these stores. Firstly, improvements in transport and communications have made it profitable to establish large-scale retail outlets in densely populated areas, particularly in city centres which attract shoppers from a wide catchment area. Secondly, manufacturing productive capacity has increased enormously, achieving not only product variety but lower unit costs and economies of scale which can be passed on to the retailer and ultimately the consumer. Thirdly, there has been a succession of departmental store acquisitions, mergers and take-overs; increased capital has been available and rationalization and modernization has followed. The stores make shopping both agreeable and attractive and the additional facility of **credit availability**, either through bank credit cards or own-store budget cards, has proved to be a powerful buying stimulus. In addition, there is a wide variety of merchandise available and the shoppers are not pressed to buy.

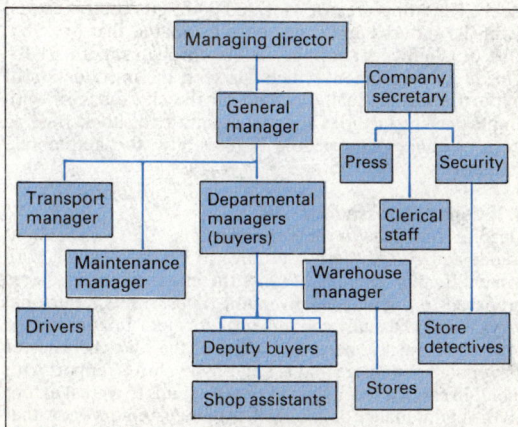

Figure 36. Department store organizational structure

Each department is run as a separate business and is under the control of a manager or buyer. Examples of department stores include Harrods, Lewis', Debenham's and Selfridge's. A typical **organizational structure** of such a store might be as shown in Figure 36.

2. Multiple shops or chain stores

These shops, several of which may be in one town, usually have identical shop fronts, layouts and features and are owned and controlled by a single business firm. Single-trade shops, as the name implies, are those which deal in one group of products, e.g. meat, shoes, dry-cleaning, etc.

Other multiples, such as Woolworths and Marks and Spencer, which abandoned the idea of a fixed price that was first experienced in the USA, usually specialize in products which are in universal and regular demand and on which they can achieve a rapid turnover. They are able to negotiate substantial discounts with manufacturers and can often insist on exclusive rights. The organization usually has a central bulk buying department – except for locally produced items and perishables – and associated warehousing and depot facilities. Apart from the advantages associated with economies of scale, the stores are invariably anxious to develop and maintain customer loyalty in other ways, for example, through product quality and reputation or variety and competitive pricing – the stores thus foster and develop a particular corporate image.

3. Supermarkets

These are large self-service stores with a floor area of over 2000 sq. ft. The emphasis tends to be on groceries and household items, although some, e.g. Tesco's, have developed clothing and DIY departments. The products which they sell are very competitively priced because of bulk buying, minimizing staffing costs and rapid turnover of stock. The stores are often located in the city centres as well as in the suburbs and it has been estimated that by 1984, 86% of all grocery shopping will be through supermarkets. This is a development which has seen the introduction of **hypermarkets**, usually located on the city outskirts with ample parking facilities and vast quantities of stock, ranging from ordinary household provisions to automobile accessories.

4. Independent traders

Despite the growth of supermarkets, the independent trader and corner shop continues to survive – albeit with some difficulty – mainly because the independent retailer is prepared to open at inconvenient times, offers a personal service and is usually conveniently located. In addition, of course, he quickly becomes aware of the idiosyncrasies of his regular customers and is able to develop a rapport with them. In essence, then, his survival depends to a great extent on the maintenance of goodwill, for his customers know that he must charge higher prices, and yet they continue to support him.

5. Mail-order businesses

Although designed originally to reach the rural markets, this method of retailing is appealing more and more to urban buyers who are able to 'shop' within the comfort of their own home, using the retailer's glossy and descriptive catalogue from which to make their selections. Although costs associated with postage and delivery, advertising and catalogue publishing are very significant, and few mail-order businesses can compete with many other forms of retail outlets as far as price is concerned, operating costs are generally lower than those of other retailers. Many mail-order businesses offer credit terms and usually all goods are sent on approval before the customer need commit himself. There are several disadvantages for the customer, including the lack of personal contact with the supplier, the limited range of stock which can be carried and the associated delivery delay. Not all products are suitable for mail-order retailing and this further restricts the range and variety of goods which can be illustrated, stocked and supplied.

Catalogues and price lists are sent frequently to either agents, who obtain commission on sales, and/or to regular customers whose addresses are recorded – particularly those customers who have a budget account with a departmental store, some of which have a mail-order organization. Despite the disadvantages, mail-order distribution is the fastest growth area in retailing and a development of this system is direct mailing – appealing to specific market segments by mailing to potential customers promotional material and order forms for a particular product.

As retailing has evolved from the *personal* service once offered to the now increasing trend towards *self-service,* manufacturers have modified their promotional and communication strategies by developing sophisticated branding and loyalty campaigns, so that retailers tend to have less influence on what products to stock because customers collectively insist on a particular brand.

Although intermediaries can be eliminated, their functions cannot, and it follows that manufacturers and producers must be aware of the idiosyncrasies of wholesaling and retailing before they can develop sound and economically rational distribution policies. To reduce channel conflict, many companies – whether manufacturing, wholesaling or retailing – are developing vertical marketing systems, e.g. Boots, the traditional chemist, has now developed into a multiple store and manufactures many of its own products.

THE FUNCTIONS OF PDM

The actual distribution of finished goods and choice of outlet is of vital importance but the other aspects of PDM must not be overlooked for they are of **equal** importance. Their relationship is depicted in Figure 37. It is impossible to turn the cogwheel of one element without all other elements being affected.

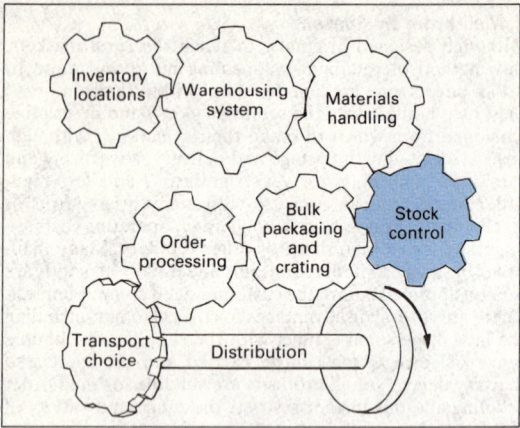

Figure 37. Physical distribution management
(Adapted from Stewart, 1965)

The systems approach is particularly relevant here for these functions are totally **interdependent** – a decision about one will certainly affect the others – which is why PDM can no more be a fragmented and uncoordinated series of activities than the major sub-systems of the company can. A factor which facilitates PDM is that most of the associated functions are **quantifiable** and therefore mathematical models for stock control, warehouse location, transportation, etc. can be constructed.

Example

A manufacturer with warehouses at A, B and C must supply retail outlets located at W, X, Y and Z. Forty lorry loads will be required, 18 from A, 10 from B and 12 from C. The retail outlets require: W – 6 loads, X – 12 loads, Y – 8 loads and Z – 14 loads. Transportation costs are proportional to the mileage involved. The geographical location of the warehouses and retail outlets and the distances involved are depicted in Figure 38.

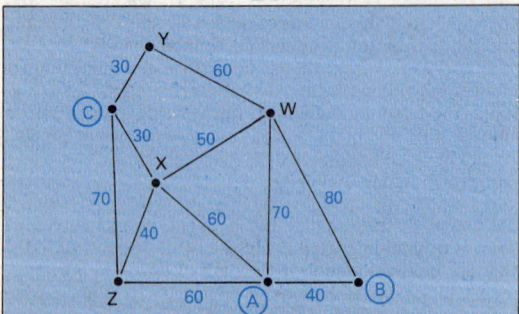

Figure 38. Warehouse: outlet locations

Decide how the lorries should be routed in order to minimize costs.

Method

Warehouse \ Outlets	W	X	Y	Z	Total
A	70 6	60	120	60 12	18
B	80	100 8	140	100 2	10
C	80	30 4	30 8	70	12
Total	6	12	8	14	40

Figure 39. Transportation matrix

Using a matrix as shown in Figure 39, allocate costs in the top right-hand corner square of each box, e.g. from warehouse A to outlet W is 70 miles. Then allocate lorry loads, attempting to achieve the lowest possible cost as follows:

In this first trial, the cost is:

$$\begin{aligned} &(6 \times 70) + (12 \times 60) = 1140 \\ +\ &(8 \times 100) + (2 \times 100) = 1000 \\ +\ &(4 \times 30) + (8 \times 30) = 360 \\ &\text{Total} \quad 2500 \text{ miles} \end{aligned}$$

This solution may not be the optimum one, i.e. the one which achieves the lowest cost within certain constraints. Numerical techniques (discussed in *Operational Research* in this series) have been developed to ensure optimization but even trial and error will quickly determine whether lower costs are possible.

The primary objective of PDM is that it must ensure an effective **flow system** from suppliers to manufacturer and from manufacturer to intermediaries at the **lowest possible cost** commensurate with an efficient service, which will neither delay nor impair the production process or increase the lead time. To this end, it is inappropriate to attempt to reduce the costs of an *individual* function of PDM, without considering the effect on the other elements, i.e. the total-system cost approach must be used. The efficiency and cost-effectiveness of PDM as a whole hinges, almost entirely, on the efficiency and effectiveness of the **stock (inventory)** control. Stock may be an accumulation of raw materials, components, semi-finished goods and completed products. Stock-holding is expensive (opportunity cost, tied up capital, etc), but stock-outs may also be expensive (loss of goodwill, unfinished orders, delays on the production line, etc).

Holding minimum stocks might realize cash which could be
used elsewhere in the firm but the firm may not then be able
to satisfy the customer's demands as quickly as the customer
would like: he may, in consequence, go elsewhere.

Consider the following table:

Company	A	B	C	D
Activity	Construction	Engineering	Chemicals	Food
Net assets employed:	£83m	£115m	£263m	£103m
Value of stock:	£15m	£6m	£58m	£49m
Rate of stock:	18%	40%	22%	47.5%

Although the activities are totally dissimilar and, ideally,
like should be compared with like, it is apparent that
companies B and D have very high stock levels. What kind
of stock is it? Raw materials or finished goods? If the stock
has a significantly high proportion of finished goods, why
are they not moving faster? Would a marketing/promotion
campaign improve liquidity? A 1% reduction in stock
holding by D would release nearly half a million pounds and
would improve cash flow. Such a high stock might indicate
that the firm was **overtrading**, i.e. it has
insufficient working capital (current assets – current liabil-
ities) to meet the requirements of its current level of
business and, in particular, its current expenditure.

Associated closely with the problems of stock control is the
problem of servicing the customer, i.e. **the lead time**. This
is particularly significant in industrial marketing with the
provision of non-differentiated products such as chemicals,
construction materials, stationery supplies, etc. The only
advantage that a manufacturer may be able to offer is a
better customer service than his competitors. This may
require the judicious siting of depots and warehouses which
immediately escalates the costs of that service.

Stock acts as a *buffer* in the event of uneven flows. Inventory
control attempts to *minimize* the amount of stock held while
maximizing the service/delivery to the ultimate consumer
and, in the process, ensuring that production is not delayed.
British Leyland, for example, has over 7000 individual
suppliers; co-ordinating inward delivery is a significant task
for the purchasing and inventory managers. Computer
models can be formulated which take into account such
variables as Economic Order Quantity (EOQ), lead times
(i.e. the time between placing a firm order and receiving the
goods), opportunity costs of stock-holding and the costs
incurred if stock runs out.

Chapter 9

Sales Forecasting

Other aspects of the marketing function

In a book of this nature, it is inevitable that some topics must be omitted and others dealt with in only a cursory manner. However, there are several major areas remaining which require some explanation and development.

All commercial organizations must attempt to minimize **uncertainty** in order that **risk** factors may be fully exposed. The risk attaching to any proposed project will not be reduced but at least, with information, the company will be more aware of the risk factors. **Sales forecasting** attempts to estimate the probability and extent of the sales which the company might achieve at some future time, expressed in terms of number of units and total value/revenue – usually for a twelve month period. From this forecast a cascade of control procedures may then be implemented. The assessment of the performance of salesmen and of the success of the sales organization generally is made by means of **sales budgets** or by **quotas**. A budget not only attempts to forecast the sales *revenue* but also the sales *costs*. Through this budget the degree of control necessary to ensure the probable success of the marketing plans is exerted.

Sales forecasting is embarked upon for four main reasons:

1. In order to prepare a **sales budget**, including the promotional expenditure and the target groups, pricing discount factors, the extent and freedom of discretionary pricing by company representatives and, of course, to define the value of the sales.

2. To co-ordinate and plan **production scheduling** in order to cope with cyclical or seasonal demand; to pre-determine raw material and components requirements and to plan provisionally, using stock-control procedures, for their delivery; to ensure that there is sufficient skilled labour for the work available and/or to make arrangements for additional work or contracts to be undertaken during slack periods in order to maximize labour, plant and machine capacity commensurate with anticipated returns or simply in order to achieve adequate *contribution* to cover the inevitable fixed costs.

3. As a *decision-analysis tool,* e.g. in assessing a product's contribution or the degree of promotional elasticity or, using techniques such as break-even analysis, the effect on sales after projected price changes.

4. To determine and formulate long-term *strategy* and the establishment of corporate objectives.

The sales forecast, in whatever shape or form, becomes crucial for it is usually on this forecast that the company's operational and competitive plans are based: for example, the amount of working capital which is going to be required – the stock and liquidity to meet current expenditure – and from which cash flows can be projected. In addition, the final sales target can be agreed with each sales manager or product manager. If the firm espouses the principles of **management by objectives**, this sales target may be set above the sales forecast in an effort to inspire the field force to greater efforts; commission, incentives and bonuses will of course be proportional to that effort. Although, in the final analysis, the forecast will be a 'guesstimate', the degree of accuracy may be increased by considering such areas as:

1. The general **economic climate** – employment opportunities and effects on aggregate demand and discretionary incomes; price stability, fiscal and monetary controls and policy; international trends and opportunities; political and social changes.

2. Assessing the industry's **share of the market** – both national and international and the company's share of the market (Interfirm Comparisons (BIM) will be useful); the growth profile of complementary products, e.g. colour TV and VCR, or motor cars and tyre sales; the availability of substitute products; the nature of the competition and the individual tactics, weaknesses and strengths of competitors.

3. The limitations of **company resources** and capacity, e.g. plant, labour, field operatives, finance, the availability of raw materials, the distribution channels and retail outlets by geographical and/or by market segmentation.

4. The analysis of **time series** in which a series of values representing past sales over a period of time are plotted on a graph in order that trends and cyclical/seasonal variations may be identified. In addition, statistical methods such as regression and correlation analysis may be employed. However, such refinements assume that the same relationships have existed between the variables during the period under review, although such an assumption may be unrealistic.

As with any control mechanism, the sales forecast – and the sales budget arising from it – requires frequent review and modifications to functional plans, when necessary. The factors on which the forecast is prepared do change and often quite dramatically, e.g. the price of oil rose 15 times between 1973 and 1980; no-one could have foreseen those increases or that the price of oil would rise from $13 a barrel in 1978 to $35 a barrel in 1980 because of the Iranian Revolution and the subsequent reduction in supply.

INTERNATIONAL TRADE

Countries, like individuals, towns or geographical regions, tend to specialize in the production of those commodities and services in which they can be most efficient. In some cases the reason for the specialization is obvious, e.g. climate or natural resources such as minerals and oil. In the UK there is usually a surplus of **capital** relative to **manpower** and this capital is used to the greater advantage in the manufacturing industries on which the UK's visible exports depend. About 20% of the UK domestic production is exported; conversely, about 60% of the value of visible imports is made up of items such as food and raw materials. However, there has been an acceleration in imports of goods which compete directly with those produced in the UK and which are intended for consumption by the home markets. The primary reason for this increase in imported semi-finished and manufactured goods is the increasing industrialization and specialization of developing countries such as Taiwan and Korea. There has also been a significant price edge on complex products imported from sophisticated economies such as those of Japan and West Germany. With the establishment of customs unions, such as the EEC, access to increased and increasing markets has necessitated the adoption of aggressive marketing strategies in order to match the international competition.

A government usually has four primary objectives:

1. **Full employment.**
2. **Stable prices.**
3. **Economic growth.**
4. **Balance of payments equilibrium.**

Unfortunately it is difficult to achieve these objectives simultaneously and in the UK it has proved impossible. The UK must export, since it must import very many of the basic goods it requires. Yet a drive to increase exports is likely to contribute to inflationary pressure because the incomes earned in producing exports are spent in the home market (or worse, are spent on imported products) but the goods produced are sold in overseas markets. Demand for some products may therefore be high relative to supply and excess money supply may lead to **demand–pull** inflation. This in turn may lead to **cost–push** inflation (as the demand for wage increases is met) and unit costs of exports increase, reducing any price advantage which may have been present.

A devaluation of the pound sterling, as an international pricing strategy, lowers the price of exports but, of course, raises the price of imports. The pound sterling has been devalued twice, in 1949 from $4.03 to $2.80 and again in 1967 when it was reduced to $2.40.

Devaluation is usually considered as a last resort when there is a fundamental disequilibrium in the **balance of payments**. There is always the danger that other countries may devalue their currency as well. Stimulating an export drive will also be pointless if there is insufficient spare capacity among UK manufacturers to meet the anticipated foreign demand.

Marketing overseas requires a quite different approach to

that adopted for the home markets; in particular the social,
cultural, economic and political environments are usually
quite different and highly specialized knowledge of foreign
idiosyncrasies is a prerequisite. Stanton (1978) makes the
point when he cites the example of Chevrolet's car, the
Nova. Marketing it in Spain or South America might prove
difficult for in Spanish 'no va' means 'it doesn't go'.

Marketing products in another country requires a specific
sub-system within the marketing department to deal with
exports. Many smaller companies, however, export through
an **agent middleman** who possesses the necessary
expertise and contacts, and charges commission on the
value of the exports. While the procedure might be
convenient, it effectively dilutes the marketing strategy and
campaign but at the same time eliminates the need (and
costs) of an overseas sales force.

Another alternative is to grant an overseas manufacturer a
licence to produce the commodity in his own country. The
originator enjoys the royalties and retains the patent rights.
Coca-Cola is perhaps the most famous product produced
under licence in the UK.

Essentially, international marketing requires each of the
ingredients of the marketing mix to be examined in detail
and an assessment made of their suitability for the intended
market. The ingredients must be modified and adapted to
suit *local* conditions. This applies particularly to the
promotional aspects and the *communications mix,* for many
countries not only have differences in quality and quantity
of media available but also different legislative controls on
advertising.

The major problems which are likely to be encountered in
marketing across national boundaries include:

1. Language and **communication** difficulties.
2. **Foreign exchange** arrangements and international
credit (ameliorated by the Exports Credits Guarantee
Department).
3. **Political** and **cultural** differences.

However the *modus operandi* of marketing remains the
same:

> An *integrated* management approach which takes into
> account the needs of the consumer from the initial design
> stage of the product through to the final point of sale, in a
> way which is of *mutual benefit* to both the consumer and
> the manufacturer. (Wild, *The Principles of Modern
> Management.*)

Chapter 10

Case Study: Fizzy Drinks Ltd

This case study is adapted from one prepared by the London Business School by whose permission it is published in its present form. The author would like to express his gratitude to Professor J. Stopford for his helpful comments.

The case study aims to bring together the various functions within a commercial and/or industrial company and to show the relevance and importance of the marketing function. The model answer is the author's own and does not purport to be the correct solution, but rather a catalyst for further discussion between students and teacher.

THE SOFT DRINKS INDUSTRY

In 1970, the total value of the British soft drinks market was in excess of £200 millions. From 1963 through to 1969 the value of this soft drinks market had been increasing at a rate of 9.1% per annum. Within the soft drinks business there were three major product areas:

1. Concentrated soft drinks – squashes – need to be diluted before drinking.

2. Mixers – soft drinks and fruit juices – generally to be added to spirits and alcoholic drinks.

3. Carbonated soft drinks, e.g. lemonade, Coca-Cola.

By 1968, concentrated soft drinks represented 53% of the total market and unconcentrated soft drinks 46%. The market for concentrated soft drinks had grown faster than that for unconcentrated soft drinks (from 1963–9, production of unconcentrated soft drinks had grown at 4% per annum).

There were two main types of carbonated soft drinks:

1. Branded products, e.g. Schweppes, Coca-Cola, Pepsi Cola, i.e. products being sold under a manufacturer's or brand name.

2. Commodity products, e.g. lemonade, limeade, dandelion and burdock, etc. These products were not sold under a brand name, and this had resulted in fierce price competition between local drink manufacturers, with resultant narrow profit margins.

Immediately after the Second World War, there were some 2000 companies manufacturing soft drinks. By 1969, this number had been reduced to between 500 and 600, due to intense competition. Many of the companies that went out of business were small regional companies serving local markets which did not have the resources to withstand competition from the major manufacturers. Within the concentrated soft drinks market in 1968 there were four major companies controlling 55% of the market: Schweppes, Beechams, Reckitt and Colman and Unilever. For the unconcentrated soft drinks market, the major market shareholders were Corona (20%), Schweppes (10%), Coca-Cola (8%), Pepsi Cola (7%), CWS (6%), Whites (5%) and Tizer (3–4%). Most of the major companies retailed their products on a national basis. With their large financial resources, they were in a position to invest in the latest high-speed bottling plants, as well as in advertising and promotion. In the retail chains and supermarkets this gave them a significant advantage against the local manufacturers in competing for shelf space.

Sales of soft drinks had traditionally been made through local, corner-shop, retail outlets. However, during the 1960s, the pattern of demand had significantly changed with the advent of supermarkets, chain and self-service stores. National chain stores and supermarkets were able to buy in bulk from the major soft drinks manufacturers, to the disadvantage of the small local manufacturers. The small local manufacturer had difficulty in serving the national chain, and also in competing on price with the major soft drinks manufacturers in bulk ordering. Off-licences had also been a traditional retail outlet for the soft drinks manufacturers. Acquisition by brewing companies of soft drinks manufacturers had, however, resulted in many of the off-licences being tied to the brewers' products. Thus the opportunities for small manufacturers to gain access to the high-volume retail outlets (with the consequent lowering of distribution costs) had been limited.

Immediately prior to 1970 there had also been significant changes in the type of packaging used for the products. Supermarkets and chain stores did not want returnable bottle sales. The result was an expansion in the use of cans, plastic cup drinks and one-trip bottles; production of cans for soft drinks increased from 300 million units in 1967 to 450 million units in 1970, and sales of soft drinks in one-trip bottles increased from 180 million units in 1968 to 363 million units in 1970. Furthermore, the use of more up-to-date materials in packaging led to changes in the package design and in the advertising carried on the packages.

FIZZY DRINKS LTD (PRE 1970)

Fizzy Drinks Ltd was founded in 1933 as a manufacturer of soft drinks. Over the years the company grew and established itself as a major manufacturer of carbonated soft drinks sold in returnable bottles. By the early 1960s, it was operating 21 depots spread across the country. These regional depots combined both production and regional sales departments in all but one of the depots.

In 1969 the firm's major products were still the carbonated

soft drinks. These products were sold in three different sizes of returnable bottles, viz. 6 oz., 25 oz., and 40 oz. The company also manufactured a line of concentrated cordials in order to enter the fast expanding concentrated soft drinks market. A franchise agreement had recently been made with the American Royal Crown Cola Company to permit the firm to enter the cola market, which represented over 20% of the UK carbonated soft drinks market. The firm did not produce soft drinks in cans or paper cups and nearly all sales of carbonated drinks were in returnable bottles. The company had invested approximately £1 million in bottles and boxes.

The company operated on a regional basis. Each depot/branch operated within an assigned geographic territory. Each branch manager was in charge of a production facility, a storage facility, a group of van drivers/salesmen, a fleet of vehicles and administrative staff. Most of the managers were men who had originally been van drivers/salesmen and had risen through the ranks to assume their current positions.

Because no one branch manufactured a full product line, it was necessary to trunk products by lorry from one branch to another to try to maintain adequate supplies at each branch. Trunking became very critical each summer at the height of the seasonal demand, to prevent stock-outs and loss of sales. The production equipment at the branches was, in many cases, quite old and of an incompatible design with modern bottling equipment. Therefore the branches were dependent on the head office engineering departments for parts and major servicing overhauls.

The company operated on a regional basis. Each depot/branch operated within an assigned geographic territory. Each branch manager was in charge of a production facility, supplying retail outlets. Selling was undertaken at each branch by a team of van drivers/salesmen who sold direct to retail outlets. Fizzy Drinks Ltd had traditionally sold to the small retail outlets and each driver had his own route and accounts to which he sold. Sales were made to the retailers either on a direct cash transaction or a credit sale basis, by the van driver/salesman. The tasks of the salesman included loading the vehicle, making rounds, checking the takings at the branch on completion of the rounds, checking the remaining stocks on the lorry and off-loading empties collected on the round. The van driver/salesmen were paid commission on sales; different products had different commission rates which could be adjusted depending on whether any particular product was being promoted.

The operating performance of the company deteriorated through the 1960s. While sales turnover had remained nearly constant at £3 million per annum since 1961, profitability fell from 1963 onwards. In 1969, profit after tax fell drastically from £133 355 to £29 986 (see Exhibit 2). At this stage, representatives of an institutional shareholder intervened and insisted that a new managing director be found from outside the company.

It was felt that a staff of 1375 people should be producing more than £3 million sales. Sundry debts had been allowed to increase from £212 206 in 1967 to £288 933 in 1968 in a period of declining sales. The company also had a very high level of liquid assets, which could have been invested elsewhere to reduce the operating costs. The level of depreciation of the fixed assets at approximately 66% suggested that much of the equipment was fairly old, even without knowing the firm's method of depreciation. Why were some of the liquid assets not being invested in equipment to spur sales? In the reserves and surplus six reserves were being held, as against the three one would expect to find, i.e. capital, revenue, P & L. The number of reserves suggested either little financial faith in the business or a lack of planning. Dividend and sales promotion expenses should be deducted out of current profitability rather than out of past profit. (Exhibits 3 and 4 provide financial details for 1967 and 1968.)

Looking at the fixed assets, there were no indications of their true value. However, it was assumed that if the plant and equipment was not worth as much as stated, then the property was worth more. Hence, the net worth of the company was probably reasonably represented. Even so, half the net worth of the company was in property and the return on assets was down to 4%. The company was making no use of debt and all these factors indicated that the company's assets were lying fallow while the plant was running down. The money should have been in working capital, transport and bottling equipment. There was, moreover, no shortage of assets to turn the company around with. Some of the comments in the chairman's report raised serious questions.

From an external analysis, it was considered that the firm had a major strength in the market awareness of the **brand** name. However, from a marketing angle, the real growth areas were in non-returnable bottles, cans, squashes and the multiple stores. The firm was not pursuing any of these areas. The firm, as a public company, had 4000 shareholders, and to the shareholders this clearly meant involvement in financial public relations work. There was an obvious need to convince the shareholders that the firm was worth sticking with. The public relations work would also have to be redesigned to have a secondary appeal to the trade. There was undoubtedly a strong and growing feeling in the trade that Fizzy Drinks Ltd was a dead company, and that there wasn't any point in continuing to buy from it because it was going out of existence. It would be necessary to create more confidence in the company so that buyers would feel it was going to stay in business and that it would be worth supporting.

Another new area was in terms of labour relations. Almost

100% of the firm's employees were members of unions and the unions were fairly militant. The firm had had a very sorry record of strikes and industrial strife, particularly within the sales organization.

Fizzy Drinks Ltd, as a company, lined up much more with the local competitors. It was, in effect, a series of 20 or so branches, all of which were small local operators rather than a cohesive national company operating in a similar manner to Coca-Cola or Corona. Coca-Cola seemed to have identified with the satisfaction area of soft drinks; what sells Coca-Cola is not that it is a better soft drink but the whole aura around the product. Corona, in contrast, does not have the same image but its strength lies in a much greater national identity, an efficient network, central objectives and standard operating methods – in other words, a rational, national approach to the business.

Fizzy Drinks Limited – Exhibit 1.
Excerpts from Extel Card (up-dated to 26.5.70)

Mineral Water and Cordial Manufacturers

The company was formed to acquire the following businesses which were engaged in the manufacture and distribution of mineral waters, botanic beers, cordials, non-alcoholic wines and vinegar. The company has an agreement with Royal Crown Cola Company of Columbus, Georgia, to bottle and sell Royal Crown Cola in Great Britain.

Sub companies: Hampshire Mineral Water Co. Ltd (Mineral Water Manufacturers); Our Boys Mineral Water Co. Ltd and Rider Wilsons Table Waters Ltd (ceased to trade during 1969); Hills Chapman Ltd (property company).

Directors: F. Hindle (chairman); P. Quinn (managing director); L. Hilton; E. Taylor; B.H.A. Taylor; G. Wilkinson; K.H.J. Hammer, MBE, E.D.

Consolidated profit and loss account

Year ended Dec. 31	Turnover £000	Divs. & int. recd. £	Net profit before tax £	Total tax £	Net profit after tax £
1960	a*	27 065	494 542	231 139	263 403
1961	a	33 104	619 571	303 381	316 190
1962	a	30 048	480 596	219 405	261 191
1963	a	31 853	598 160	293 561	304 599
1964	a	36 727	567 471	246 646	320 825
1965	a	47 047	438 588	134 967	303 621
1966	a	45 194	443 760	171 421	272 339
1967	a	41 682	361 112	157 551	203 561
1968	2984	41 810	231 840	98 485	133 355
1969	2949	47 657	60 111	30 125	29 986

Year ended Dec. 31	% on ordinary less tax		Retained profit for year	Depn	Av. no. empl's
	Earned	Paid	£	£	
1960	43.0 Int 7.5 Fin 17.5 Bon	2.5	94966	87747	a
1961	51.6 Int 7.5 Fin 17.5 Bon	2.5	147753	92585	a
1962	42.6 Int 7.5 Fin 17.5 Bon	2.5	92753	98398	a
1963	49.7 Int 7.5 Fin 17.5 Bon	7.5	105537	136135	a
1964	54.3 Int 7.5 Fin 17.5 Bon	17.5	69262	131304	a
1964	39.5				
1965	30.4 Int 7.5 Fin 17.5 Bon	2.5	e28621	131746	a
1966	27.3 Int 7.5 Fin 17.5 Bon	2.5	M 2661	133304	a
1967	20.4 Int 7.5 Fin 17.5		M 6439	122093	a
1968	13.3 Int 7.5 Fin 7.5		M16645	102609	kl360
1969	3.0 Int Nil Fin 7.5		M45014	92181	kl360

*Excluding purchase tax: a not disclosed; e dividends deducted gross (income tax retained £30 937); j estimated earnings after allowing for corporation tax at 40%; k remuneration £1 038 000 in 1968, and £1 126 000 in 1969.

Directors' interests in ordinary shares of the company at 31.12.69: beneficial, 15 941; as trustees, 850 000.

London prices of 5/- ordinary shares

Cal. Year	1961	1962	1963	1964	1965	1966	1967	1968	1969	*1970
Highest	26/6	25/6	29/9	27/9	27/9	24/10	26/7	24/3	21/9	11/9
Lowest	20/4	20/-	20/3	21/4	22/-	14/3	16/1	17/1	6/9	8/3

*To May 18th

Net asset value (book value), excluding intangibles, at B/s. date per 5/- Ordinary share: 1969, 11/-

Land and buildings The value of land and buildings is substantially in exess of book value and valuations made since 31 December 1969 indicate that this excess could be in the region of £5 000 000 on the open market. As a major part is used for the trading company, however, it is the opinion of the directors that the current open market value is not of great significance in the context of these accounts.

Chairman's statement

Trading results are disappointing as the directors had hoped to achieve an increased turnover. Failure of this kind, and a fall in the Group's total gross sales value by £35 000, can be specifically attributed to a number of factors:

1. A policy of rationalization of manufacturing, by closure or reduction to distribution points of certain units. This applied particularly to closure of their branch in Glasgow due to an increasing non-profitability which had applied for some years in spite of changes in management. Certain smaller branches in the North East and in South Wales were closed or consolidated for the same reason.

2. Inability during exceptional weather in June and July (when they were able to trade at full production for the first time for some years) to recoup the general fall during poor winter months at the beginning of the year.

3. A price increase granted by the Ministry last August which for a time met sales resistance in certain areas.

In addition, account must be taken of increasing encroachment into the family soft drinks market of American brands of Cola products.

Fall in profit, however, overtook the amount lost in turnover due to persistent rises in labour, materials and operating and marketing costs during the year, which had to be absorbed by the company. Both turnover and profit suffered from labour unrest while changed regulations in Selective Employment Tax (S.E.T.) alone cost the company £20000. An additional charge for packaging costs was sustained despite reduction in volume of output, although to a minor extent this was offset by an increased deposit charge on the 40 oz. size bottle. An outstanding item of expense was the substantial increase in the cost of transport, aggravated by new regulations imposed by the Road Transport Act of 1968. Return to profitability depends upon the company's ability to contain or pass on these extra costs.

The board of directors have given continual consideration to product innovations – in view of the reduction in the number of trips of returnable bottles and to the extension of marketing operations including the use of non-returnable bottles. During the latter part of 1969, a pilot operation in this type of outlet was started and in the present year sales to multiple stores and supermarkets are being extended. It is, as yet, too early to forecast the level of success and profitability of these operations in such a highly competitive market.

As American branded Cola accounts for approximately 25% of all carbonated drinks sold in the UK, a decision was taken during the latter part of 1969 to enter the competition in this field. The company subsequently negotiated a franchise agreement to bottle and market, in Great Britain, Royal Crown Cola, and the company has now commenced producing this Cola. Last year, development of a new major production unit was proposed. In view of the large capital commitment required by this project, the company is now considering the matter again before proceeding any further.

Exhibit 2.
Consolidated balance sheet as at 31 December 1968

1967 £		£	£
	Share capital		
	Authorised 6 000 000		
1 500 000	ordinary shares of 5/- each	1 500 000	
	Issued 4 000 000		
	ordinary shares of 5/-		
	each,		
1 000 000	fully paid		1 000 000
	Reserves		
12 201	Capital	26 652	
1 000 000	Revenue	1 000 000	
75 000	Dividend equalization	75 000	
40 000	Sales promotion	25 000	
60 000	Taxation equalization	60 000	
167 325	Profit and loss account	170 673	
1 354 526			1 357 325
2 354 526	**Total capital and reserves**		2 357 325
	Fixed assets (see note)		
886 580	Land and buildings		823 153
547 828	Plant, machinery and		530 849
	motor vehicles		
1 438 408			1 354 002
	Current assets		
409 711	Stock in trade	361 631	
240 309	Sundry debtors and	323 481	
	amounts prepaid British		
	government and other		
	securities		
232 174	(Market value £228 894–	232 174	
	1967 £221 552)		
475 000	Municipal and other	475 000	
	deposits		
241 446	Cash at bankers and in	179 832	
	hand		
1 598 640		1 572 118	
	Deduct: **current liabilities**		
247 048	Sundry creditors and	293 583	
	amounts accrued		
157 894	Current taxation	155 592	
175 000	Provision for final	75 000	
	dividend (gross) now		
	recommended		
579 942		524 175	
1 018 698	**Net current assets**		1 047 943
2 453 106			2 401 945

£	Deduct: **deferred liability**	£
157170	Corporation tax due 1 January 1970	103210
2295936		2298735
	Add: **goodwill** at cost less amounts written off including net premiums on shares acquired in subsidiary	
58590	companies	58590
2354526	**Total net assets**	2357325

Note on accounts

1. Fixed assets	1968	1967
Land and buildings	£	£
At cost 1 January 1968	684020	650370
At valuation	369418	369418
	1053438	1019788
Additions during the year at cost	13424	44059
Less: disposal during the year	69195	10409
	997667	1053438
Cumulative depreciation	174514	166858
At net book value 31 Dec. 1968	823153	886580
Freehold	740003	800338
Leasehold	83150	86242
	823153	886580

Plant, machinery and motor vehicles	1613937	1607275
Additions during the year at cost	92672	61820
Less: disposal during the year	167150	55156
	1539459	1613939
Cumulative depreciation	1008610	1066111
At net book value 31 Dec. 1968	530849	547828

Exhibit 3.
Consolidated profit and loss account: year ended 31 December 1968

1967 £		£	£
468549	Trading profit on the year		308249
–	Add: profit arising on change of stocktaking basis		18291
1966	Profit on sales of properties		8433
470515			334973
	Add: investment income:		
9540	Investments	10067	
32142	Cash on deposit	31743	
41682			41810
512197			376783

£	Deduct:	£	£
122 093	Depreciation of fixed assets	102 609	
2 818	Losses on sales of fixed assets	5 139	
25 520	Directors' remuneration	27 790	
1 506	Other miscellaneous charges	6 111	
151 937			141 649
360 260	Profit of the year subject to taxation.		235 134
152 443	Deduct: taxation on profit of year		96 786
207 817	Profit of the year after taxation		138 348
174 508	Add: balance brought forward from previous year		167 325
35 000	Add: transfer from sales promotion reserve		15 000
417 325			320 673
	Deduct: share dividends		
75 000	Interim 7½% (gross) already paid	75 000	
175 000	Final 7½% (gross) now recommended	75 000	
250 000			150 000
	Balance carried forward		
167 325	next year		170 673

CASE STUDY ANALYSIS

The study will take the form of an initial analysis by functional areas and will demonstrate their inter-relationship. Further, it will emphasize the need for an integrated systems approach to the study of organizational strategy and decision-making.

CORPORATE PLANNING

1. It seems almost incredible that in the face of relatively simple accounting procedures, which clearly showed a declining profit from 1965 onwards, the firm's board of directors appeared not to implement or even plan constructive marketing and financial tactics or strategy. In spite of a fast growing market of 9.1% for all soft drinks (4% p.a. for carbonated and 13% for concentrates), they appeared to be complacent with a consistent sales turnover of approximately £3 million.

2. The major objective of Fizzy Drinks Ltd should have been to **maintain their market share**, which necessitated increasing their turnover by 9.1% p.a., and to increase the volume of sales.

3. There appears to be a complete dearth of company

objectives, even regional or branch management objectives. If objectives were defined, then they were either pitched too high or the firm lacked the management expertise to quantify these objectives, both at board and branch levels.

4. In general, at this time, in the soft drinks industry new products were being launched, particularly in non-returnable containers, yet the firm invested **£1 million in returnable** bottles and crates. Supermarkets and large chain stores did not want the problem of returnable containers nor did they want to lose valuable warehouse space by stocking empty bottles, or refunding deposits on bottles at busy checkouts. (The IPC manual forecast that by 1980, 86% of all groceries would be sold in supermarkets – yet the firm's main outlet was in the small retail business.) They appeared to be unaware of the change in marketing methods.

5. Although they had an almost national distribution network, their distribution costs must have been enormous, particularly as they were trunking to different regions. Clearly, there was a need to rationalize the production organization, with a view to **centralizing** at comparatively few centres and possibly achieving **economies of scale** by reducing labour costs, overheads and distribution costs. A relatively simple transportation study would have revealed a more economical and efficient method of trunking, even if some of their dilapidated vehicle fleet were sold in favour of large articulated lorries.

6. It was apparent that, in most other areas of the industry, the traditional returnable bottle was being replaced very quickly by cans, plastic containers and non-returnable bottles. Investment in a high speed canning plant would appear to have been a logical step, particularly as the cans carried with them the opportunity of greatly increased advertising and brand image exposure.

7. What business was the firm in? Ostensibly carbonated drinks, concentrates and road haulage. What was their *intended* strategy? There appears to have been no explicit statement of strategy nor any statement of tactics which might have been used as a basis for competitive success. The critical competitive arena within which their tactics should have been formulated include:

(a) Returnable/non-returnable bottle sales.
(b) Increase in market outlets.
(c) Sales by market segmentation.
(d) Full exploitation of 21 distribution outlets as a *cohesive* organization rather than a collection of fragmented units.
(e) Development of company strength, notably national distribution network and brand image.
(f) Renegotiation of franchise for Cola which was priced on a fixed return basis and not on sales revenue.
(g) Improvement of management expertise at all levels. The top management appears to lack co-ordinating ability and has evolved with the company but is not familiar with modern commercial management techniques.

FINANCIAL ANALYSIS

Ratio	1967	1968	Remarks
1. Liquidity (a) Acid test $\dfrac{\text{Bank} + \text{debtors}}{\text{Creditors} + \text{taxation}}$	1.19:1	1.12:1	Able to meet its immediate commitments (but consider debt time below– increasing).
(b) **Current** Current assets	2.76:1	2.99:1	Working capital is increasing (although stocks have *decreased*) but *no* increase in sales. Too much liquidity. Raw materials relatively cheap. Assets not being fully employed. Fixed overhead costs still have to be met.
(c) Fixed assets/ total capital used	22.5%	23.2%	Interfirm Comparisons required.
2. Performance ratios (a) Turnover/total capital	1.27	1.25	Decreasing, but carbonates growing at 3% p.a. and concs. at 13% p.a.
(b) Working capital/ sales	0.78	0.78	Static but market is *expanding*.
(c) Return on net current assets (working capital)	19.9%	12.7%	Investigation of overhead costs; manufacturing costs; pricing policy; turnover; standard costing; budgetary control.
(d) $\dfrac{\text{Gross profit margin}}{\text{Gross profit/sales}}$	12%	7.7%	(1969–2%) Increased costs, i.e. labour, distribution.
(e) $\dfrac{\text{Fixed assets}}{\text{Sales/F.A.}}$	£2.09:1	£2.2:1	Fixed asset disposals substantially increased for 1968, reducing total F.A.
(f) Fixed asset utilization (per £000 of sales). Plant/MC/vehicles/land and buildings	£7.7 £3.72	£5.3 £3.32	Chronic underutilization of fixed assets
(g) Rate of stock T/O, sales/stock	7.3 times per year. 50 days	8.2 (44 days)	Less stock held in 1968 but sales are *down*. Less production in 1968. Requirement for forecasting techniques.
(h) Debtors T/O, sales/debts	12.4 × (29 days)	9.2 × (40 days)	Terms of payment–30 days. Debt time increasing in time of falling sales and profits? Credit control linked to invoicing? Bad debts. Are most sales for cash via van drivers?
(i) Stock/NCA (net current assets)	40%	35%	
3. Gearing Shareholders capital/total capital	1:2.3	1:2.3	Although low geared, no advantage taken of possibility of dividend changes or reductions as a step towards capital investment.
(a) Sales/share capital	3:1	3:1	No improvement, although market for soft drinks increasing at 9.1% p.a.
4. Sales per employee	£2205	£2205	Rising costs, falling sales but no increase in turnover and/or production.

FINANCIAL ANALYSIS cont'd

Ratio	1967	1968	Remarks
5. Earnings Ratios (a) Net profit/Equity	20%	13%	Falling but market expanding. Rising costs; declining value
(b) Profit after tax/total capital	8.6%	5.6%	
(c) Profit before tax/total assets	15.3%	9.8%	

Interpretation

There are numerous financial and management ratios. The most important have already been cited.

It is, however, necessary to remember that ratios essentially indicate *trends* – a single ratio is of limited value.

As the balance sheets for 1967 and 1968 only are given, it must be borne in mind that the ratios will not necessarily be diagnostic. Equally, a great deal of useful information is missing such as overhead costs, distribution costs and sales turnover before 1967 (believed to be about £3 million).

The Economic Development Council did not, at this time, maintain statistics for the soft drinks industry, so it might well have proved difficult to obtain figures about comparable organizations.

General observations

1. An improvement in the **Return on Capital Employed** (ROCE) must be a central point in the company's objectives. There must be separation of unused or insufficiently used assets such as land or buildings and the realization of them. However, the tax implications must be studied carefully so that excessive tax repayments are not concomitant with 'stripping'.

2. The long-term planning must be concerned with the question of the application of money derived from depreciation and the retained profits – *but* they already possess an excess of liquidity which is lying relatively fallow.

3. Production costs, notably labour, overheads and marketing costs, are rising; concentrating on one (or more) *major* production unit might significantly reduce production costs and help centralize production activity, achieving possible economies of scale.

4. The cash available in the business should be used as effectively as possible. There appears to be a **large surplus of funds** over and above the requirements for current production and selling.

Current assets are proportionately high. In 1968 they totalled £1 210 487.

It is probable that the invested funds are relatively long-term investments as a hedge against fluctuations in trade, but they could probably be easily realizable; it may indicate, however, a management structure unwilling (or unable) to take risks and a **conservative and cautious leadership**.

There are other points concerning the invested income:

(a) It is only realizing 5.9% gross interest. (Is it therefore short-term investment at 2% below 1968 bank rates?)
(b) The purchasing power of the investment is not being maintained (inflation).
(c) It is gilt-edged (conservative management?).
(d) Considering the apparent need for the company to invest in new plant and vehicles, to markedly increase its advertising expenditure and adopt an aggressive sales policy and to indulge in more specific, definitive market research, the money has not been invested in the best interests of the business stakeholders – the shareholders, management, employees and customers.
(e) Business experience shows that companies in general tend *not to remain static nor stagnate*, but go either forwards or backwards. Even a policy of internal expansion is a progressive forward move yet the firm does not appear to have adopted any part of this strategy.

5. The regular 7.5% half-yearly dividend gives the appearance of stability. It might have attracted potential investors if capital for plant renewal and expansion was contemplated, particularly as they have only issued two thirds of their authorized shares.

6. The working capital is high and could indicate:

(a) Inefficient use of current assets.
(b) Lack of control over labour performances.
(c) Inefficient storekeeping and too many finished goods (but consider the danger of stock-outs and shelf-life of soft drinks).
(d) Fixed assets are not being replaced and therefore become expensive to maintain and operate.

7. Although the organization chart on page 116 shows a financial director and an assistant accountant it does not indicate that there is a finance department and it is doubtful that a central one exists. Attached to this department should be a cost-accounting section. The company's major objective appeared to be to satisfy the shareholders at the expense of everything else – even to withdrawing large sums from reserves for four years in order to meet the dividend payments.

8. There is a constant requirement to compare the accounting ratios with those of similar companies using the Centre for Inter-Firm Comparisons (CIFC). There is no indication that this was in fact done and if it *was* done, then no corrective/remedial measures appear to have been taken. If comparisons from CIFC were not available, Extel or Moodies' cards could have been used.

9. Each branch manager appears to have been financially autonomous. **Decentralization** is fine, providing that each unit becomes a *profit centre* with definite goals and financial constraints as part of the overall financial plan of the organization.

10. A **gap analysis** between the annual turnover achieved, and the annual growth of the carbonated, concentrated and total soft drinks markets, shows a divergent turnover realization. This trend was apparent well before the profits began to fall substantially, and was an indication that even if production and distribution facilities were not improved there was a real and definite need for an *aggressive* sales policy to run coincidentally with a positive advertising campaign.

It makes sense to sell hidden reserves to finance expansion particularly in the firm's case because the potential expansion of the firm could be distinctly profitable.

11. Labour costs have risen 8.5%.
Average annual wage: 1967 – £763
1968 – £827
They also account for 34% (1967) and 50% (1968) of the sales turnover.

Notes from the consolidated profit and loss account

1. Reduction in trading profit
by £160300. Why?

	468549
Sales remain approximately the same –	308249
therefore costs rising? Labour? Overheads?	£160300

2. Total profit from undertaking down by
£135544. (Investment income
remains about the
same at £41000.)

	470515
	334973
	£135542

3. Trading profit reduced by 34%. What was the change in stock valuation method to realize £18291?

4. Depreciation of land and buildings? Presumably lease-hold disposal (or possibly very old buildings?). Lower fixed asset value; higher accumulative depreciation? Indication of change of method used to calculate depreciation.

5. No debentures, therefore no charge against profits. No preference shares, therefore no appropriation of profits.

Fund flow analysis	1968
Sources, Internal	
Profit before taxation	376783
Depreciation charges	102609

Variations in working capital

Increase in creditors	46535
Decrease in stocks	48080
Decrease in debtors	
	574007

Applications

Internal

Purchase of fixed assets	5139

External:

Nil

Payments

Dividends	150000
Taxation	96786
Directors' remuneration	27790
Miscellaneous	6111

Variations in working capital

Increase in debtors	83172

Summary

Increase in assets	205009

Financial implications: Conclusions

1. Rapidly declining return on capital employed.
2. Liquidity greatly in excess of requirements.
3. Little evidence of financial planning, budgetary control or standard costing.
4. An apparently blinkered attitude of paying the equity dividends at all costs, probably caused by a need to maintain the shareholders' confidence in the face of decline in company performance.
5. Gap analysis indicates a dramatic fall in the company's share of the soft drinks market.
6. Labour intensive firm with decreasing utilization of fixed assets.
7. 'If an acceptable long-term return cannot be achieved, it is better to liquidate the firm and invest the capital elsewhere' (Bruno Hake, *Business Strategy and Planning*).

PRODUCTION

1. Production facilities were available at 20 of the depots but the full range was *not* manufactured at any *single* unit. This might indicate insufficient plant but on the other hand full utilization of plant was only achieved in 1969. Presumably each depot or group of depots produced a specific range which necessitated long haulage and heavy transportation costs. The fixed asset utilization indicates a definite decline. The organization was labour intensive – albeit that many of their employees were part-time women – and had suffered industrial unrest, particularly by the van drivers/salesmen.

2. The plant and vehicles were highly depreciated, indicating old and obsolete equipment. Major engineering work was only completed by head office engineers. Breakdowns would therefore necessitate an expensive waiting time. It appears that little effort was made to innovate with modern technological developments.

3. Installation of centralized production facilities (at say, 3 or 4 regions) while being a major capital investment, unless involving use of leased plant, would have reduced manufacturing costs considerably and would have drastically reduced the requirement for frequent trunking – particularly if contract haulage had been used – and the intensive labour requirements. Distribution of raw materials to a few plants would have been easier. The new production plants – with an excess capacity of say 20–30% to meet growth requirements and demand fluctuations – would have ensured continuous flow production.

4. Purchase or lease of high-speed canning plants would not only have released staff from the cleaning and control of returnable bottles, but would also have provided a valuable source of cheap advertising and public saturation of the brand image through packaging promotion.

5. The firm relied on a very high volume of output to earn the desired level of profit. The principal reasons for this were a large total of fixed overheads and a relatively small rate of profit per £1 of sales.

6. The branch managers should have informed higher management if the production capacity variance changed because plant was idle due to trade recession, machinery breakdowns or labour disputes. The importance of defining the capacity is vital. Unless the branch managers clearly understand the number of standard hours, the number of units, the value of sales or other measures, there can be no effective control of performances or overhead costs.

PROVISIONING AND STOCK CONTROL

– Raw materials stock.
– Retailing stock.

1. These two types of stock would be held by 20 of the depots. A comprehensive and efficient feedback to head office would be necessary to maintain an accurate reflection of the total stock held – possibly using computer network or bureau or daily phone-ins.

2. Centralization of raw material stocks to the major production units would rationalize stock-holding and purchasing requirements and facilitate PDM.

3. There was a definite danger that stock-outs could occur and lead time increase by producing at 20 depots while not producing the full range at each depot.

4. There might well have been a case for producing more exclusive drinks with concomitant higher returns, e.g. champagne perry.

5. At December 31 the stock was sufficient to last for only 43 days. Raw materials – except perhaps sugar – are cheap. Also, before 1969 the company had invested in £1 million worth of bottles and crates. Were these fully utilized?

MARKETING AND SALES

1. Use of market research

(a) Soft drinks business

1945–2000 ⎫
          ⎬ 62 firms went out of business each year.
1969–500 ⎭

(b) Four companies produced 55% concentrates. Seven companies produced 60% carbonated, but Fizzy Drinks Ltd held only 4% of this.

(c) Growth in canned drinks   – 17% p.a. (67–70)
               one-trip bottles – 51% p.a. (68–70)
(IPA statistics)

2. Market growing at 9.1% p.a. but the firm's share failed to grow with the market. Supermarket growth – bulk buying in cans or one-trip bottles – brought a new dimension. No effort was made to enter the cans or one-trip bottle market; traditional retail outlets and methods were adhered to.

3. Price rises in the firm's product and an increase in the deposit on bottles led to sales resistance and a further decline in sales. Yet market changes made it doubly imperative to introduce more effective selling techniques.

4. The firm needed to reduce the level of calling on the many smaller outlets while improving service to the fewer but larger shops. Research into the market would have established patterns and trends and the main weight of selling, effort and time could be concentrated where the potential was greatest.

5. The following possible sales tactics should have been investigated:

(a) Alternative outlets, e.g. wholesalers, chain stores.
(b) Re-organization of sales territories to give salesmen an equal load based upon sales potential.
(c) Revision of commission schemes.
(d) Use of linear programming to determine optimum allocation of resources to meet conflicting demands.
(e) Possible use of computer packages for transportation, vehicle scheduling and depot siting.
(f) Identification of highest profitability on sales by products, customers, geographical areas.
(g) Packaging: use of palletization, disposables, customer acceptability.
(h) Sales forecasting by region and subsequent sales budgeting was imperative.

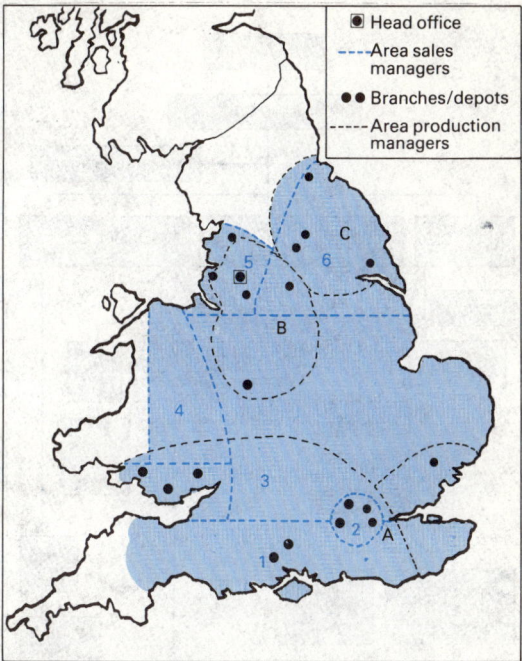

Figure 40. Fizzy Drinks distribution network

Notes to Figure 40

1. There is a paucity of branches in the South West and South East.
2. There is no representation at all in the North West and Scotland.
3. Overlap of responsibilities of area sales managers and area production managers.
4. Are the branches/depots located in the highest or potentially highest sales areas?
5. Consider the requirement to trunk, particularly to the densely populated Midlands.

ORGANIZATIONAL STRUCTURE

1. The branches/depots were fragmented units instead of forming a cohesive multicellular organization. It was therefore difficult to act in **unison** to obtain market penetration. Most of the branch managers had originally been van drivers/salesmen; there was therefore a chronic **dearth of management expertise**. Decentralization, or delegation of responsibility for achieving results, enables decisions to be made by managers who are closer to the product and the market, and who have a greater relevant specialist knowledge. This assumes that the managers are

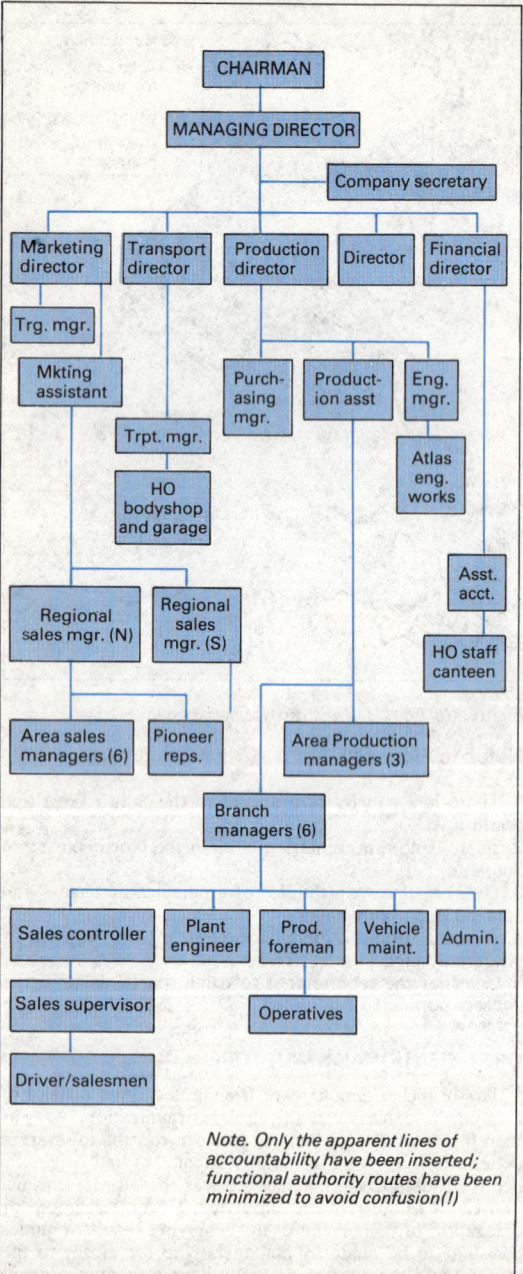

Note. Only the apparent lines of
accountability have been inserted;
functional authority routes have been
minimized to avoid confusion(!)

Figure 41. Fizzy Drinks – organizational structure

capable not only of *analysing* information but can also provide *quality* of feedback to top management and not just quantity.

Metamorphosis of the depots into **profit centres** might have made branch managers more profit conscious, relieving top management from routine work and allowing them to develop strategies for the *enterprise as a whole*.

2. There was a sorry record of **industrial unrest** resulting in loss of production and an increase in overheads. Although a training manager is shown on the chart there is no personnel department as such.

3. There is a glut of administrative and clerical personnel relative to the size and turnover of the organization.

4. There is a need for implementing regional Management by Objectives, productivity bargaining and job descriptions and specifications, with a view to training the labour force.

5. Disadvantages of the firm's structure:

(a) Duplication of functions at branch level.
(b) Centralized bodyshop and garage.
(c) Centralized engineering function.
(d) Too many communicating links.
(e) Stratas within the structure which appear to make no significant contribution to the organization.
(f) Lack of accountability/responsibility between sales and production.
(g) No centralized cost centre.
(h) Lack of personnel function permeates through to branch level. Need for appraisal systems for recognizing potential management.
(i) Functional parochialism.

The organization restructure
Rationalization of the organizational structure will be dependent upon:

1. Reduction of production facilities to three major areas.

2. Disposal of the Atlas Engineering Company.

3. Disposal of all subsidiaries.

4. Locally contracting for *minor* (say, £100) repairs on vehicles.

5. Pool of serviceable vehicles (say, three) to be held by regional transport manager.

6. Full range of products – identified by outlet, market, customer acceptability, etc. – to be manufactured at each production centre.

7. Each branch (and region) to have a sales objective based upon potential and a volume of profit objective based upon increased sales and reduction of overheads.

8. New commission basis for salesmen *and* branch managers, say, quarterly bonus distribution scheme.

9. Importation of top management expertise – pensioning off and reducing some of the existing top management.

10. Diplomatically and with trade union co-operation, pruning the existing shop-floor labour force but in return giving payment incentives to the retained labour force.

11. Capital realization programme for plant and vehicle investment and for a saturation advertising campaign.

DIVERSIFICATION
The *less* diverse a business, the *more* manageable it is. In any diversification plan, imported management expertise would be of paramount importance. However, such expertise is expensive.

The essential point about the firm is that it must have growth in the *volume of profit* (*not* just the volume of sales) if it is to produce an acceptable return on capital employed. The primary decision must be whether or not they should stay in the industry or whether they should quit the soft drinks market and venture into new fields.

All the most salient and relevant factors concerning diversification apply to this firm, viz:

1. Technological change – packaging, high-speed automated production plant, computerization.
2. Falling demand for their products (relative to the growth of the market).
3. Surplus capital.
4. Seasonal demand.
5. Competitive pressures.

These factors indicate that there is a need for radical change.

Sale, divestment and systematic shrinkage
The firm might consider divesting itself of markets in the South West, South East and Wales, where they have relatively few distribution points, substantially reducing their overheads (relative to sales) and realizing their fixed assets for investment into new plant, particularly in the highest market outlets.

The right size is important; at present the firm is over-stretched and undertrading. '*Absolute size is not necessarily an indicator of success and achievement. The right size is.*' (Drucker, *Management.*)

Further Reading

For a more informative and discursive account, the following are strongly recommended:

Cannon, T., *Basic Marketing* (Holt, 1980)

Coyle, R.G., *Decision Analysis* (Nelson, 1972)

Crisp, R.D., *Marketing Research* (McGraw-Hill, 1957)

Etzioni, A., *Modern Organizations* (Prentice-Hall, 1964)

Giles, G.B., *Marketing* (MacDonald & Evans, 1974)

Hutton, G., *Thinking About Organizations* (Tavistock, 1972)

Johnson, S., *Marketing and Financial Control* (Pergamon Press, 1967)

Kotler, P., *Marketing Management* (Prentice-Hall, 1973)

Likert, R., *New Patterns of Management* (McGraw-Hill, 1964)

Lipsey, R.G., *An Introduction to Positive Economics* (Weidenfeld & Nicolson, 1975)

Rodger, L.W., *Marketing in a Competitive Economy* (Hutchinson, 1969)

Schwartz, G., *Science in Marketing* (Wiley, 1965)

Sofer, C., *Organizations in Theory and Practice* (Heinemann, 1973)

Stanton, C., *Fundamentals of Marketing* (McGraw-Hill, 1978)

Tinniswood, P., *Marketing Decisions* (Longman, 1981)

Worcester, R.M., *Consumer Market Research Handbook* (McGraw-Hill, 1972)

Glossary

Advertising The process of informing and persuading actual and potential consumers, through a communication method, of a product or service availability.

Advertising coverage Breadth and dimension of market segments to which the advertisement will be transmitted.

Advertising frequency The number of times an advertisement is transmitted to a particular market segment.

Agent middleman An intermediary in a channel of distribution who does not purchase the goods himself but who arranges for their delivery.

Aggregate demand The total demand for goods and services in the economy. It consists of consumer goods and services, investment goods, demand for goods by local and central governments and the demand for exports.

Aggression A behavioural response usually as a result of a frustrated goal or need and often as a defensive mechanism.

Articles of Association The internal regulations on the running of the company, which are registered when the company is formed.

Attitudes Opinions and judgements which are formed as a result of the internalized values and beliefs.

Balance of payments A table of debits and credits incurred as a result of international trade and which is divided into a capital account and a current account.

Beliefs The acceptance of something which is acknowledged as real or true.

Biogenic Relating to those needs which satisfy physiological requirements.

Brand An identifying name, logo, trademark or other characteristic.

Break-even analysis An accountancy technique which studies how revenue and costs vary with the level of output and which determines the level where total costs are exactly the same as total revenue.

Budgeting Financial planning which must have a financial objective and which takes into account factors such as cash flows and stock changes. Budgets are usually drawn up for each department in a business in order that a profit and loss account may be projected.

Capital goods Those goods which are used in the production process and which have themselves been produced. Usually divided into fixed capital and circulating capital.

Channels of distribution The route taken by the title to the goods.

Closed system An organization with impermeable boundaries which effectively blocks the inward and outward flow of information, e.g. a Tibetan monastery in the Himalayas is almost a closed system.

Cluster sampling A method of statistical sampling by considering a number of members of the total population but confined to a specific area.

Communications mix The sum total of variables through

which and by which the firm attempts to inform and persuade potential consumers to buy its product, i.e. promotion, merchandising, packaging, etc.

Competitive pricing Pricing a product or service at a price comparable with that currently charged by competitors, i.e. the going-rate.

Complementary products Goods which tend to be sold with each other, demand for one affecting demand for the other, e.g. fish and chips, cameras and flash-bulbs.

Conflict Incompatibility of some kind. In psychology it refers to a clash between wants or impulses which contradict each other.

Constraints Factors which limit or prevent a certain course of action.

Consumer A person who buys and uses goods or services.

Consumer durables Products of a domestic nature, i.e. for the household.

Consumption The expenditure on goods or services within an economy.

Contribution In cost accountancy, the amount of sales revenue remaining, to pay for fixed costs and contribute to profits after variable costs have been met.

Corporate objective The overall strategic aim, target or goal of the organization attained through corporate planning and the implementation of control procedures.

Corporation An association of persons who are recognized as having a single legal identity and so can sue or be sued.

Culture Includes all those factors and variables which are involved in an individual's socialization process, i.e. the prevailing values, beliefs, attitudes and customs within his environment.

Data Qualitative and quantitative information from either a primary and/or secondary source.

Delegation The act of entrusting a task to an individual or group. It consists of the sum total of trust and control which are inversely proportional to each other.

Demand Want for a commodity accompanied by an ability and willingness to pay for the product.

Devaluation A reduction in the value of one currency relative to the exchange value of another country's currency.

Discretionary income The amount of income which an individual has remaining after paying for vital services to maintain his standard of living and which he may therefore spend at his discretion.

Durable products Consumer goods which give satisfaction over a period of time rather than being consumed immediately, e.g. a refrigerator.

Economic growth The increase in the productive capacity of a nation and its subsequent increase in national income.

Economics The study of the way in which a society chooses to allocate scarce resources. It consists essentially of what to make, how to make it and who should get it.

Economies of scale Occur when the scale of productions is increased and as a result average unit costs fall because of economies achieved internally or externally.

Ego An individual's conscious awareness of self.

Elasticity The reaction of demand for a product to a marginal change in the price of that product. It is affected significantly by the availability of acceptable substitute products.

Environment The world which surrounds an organization or individual and which, in some way, affects and influences the individual's behaviour.

Feasible area That area bounded by the constraint relationships in a linear programming problem and in which the objective may be achieved but not necessarily optimized. Maximization or minimization of the objective will occur at the vertex furthest away from the origin.

Feedback In a communications process, it consists of the information which returns in response to an initial input from a source.

Fiscal Originating from fiscus – a Roman emperor's purse. In economics refers to governmental changes in levels and methods of direct and indirect taxation and of variations in the levels of public expenditure. It is through these two instruments that a government can basically control the level of demand in an economy.

Fixed costs The costs which remain the same in the short term such as interest payments, rates, rent, depreciation, management salaries, etc.

Forecast An attempt to quantify, in total units and sales revenue, the level of demand for a product over a period of time and from which other control techniques such as departmental budgets may be derived.

Formal organization The way in which individuals in organizations are supposed to react according to the organizationally imposed rules, regulations and procedures. It embraces such concepts as lines of authority, span of control, organizational charts, staff/line relationships, etc.

Frustration A sense or feeling of helplessness or impotence as a result of being unable to fulfil a need or goal. It may manifest itself through a display of aggression.

Full employment Occurs when everyone who wishes to work – at a given wage-rate – is doing so. However, there will always be some people who are unemployed if only because of frictional employment which occurs as a result of individuals changing their jobs.

Gearing The ratio of interest-bearing debt capital to equity (ordinary share) capital. If a company is highly geared it will have to pay high interest charges even when it is making little profit.

Gross domestic product The total of the output of goods and services produced by the economy over a period of time. Products and services are valued at market prices. It does not include intermediate products or income from overseas investments.

Imperfect market An economic market situation in which the products for sale are not homogeneous, where there are few buyers and sellers and where there are barriers to entry.

Impulse purchasing Consumer buying phenomenon in which no premeditated decision to purchase has been made, i.e. bought on the spur of the moment.

Income The money which accrues to an individual or organization either from investments or the sale of some service, e.g. labour—wages. It should be differentiated from revenue.

Industrial market The market for capital goods or intermediate products used in the manufacture of finished products or which help a company to meet its obligations.

Inference The practice of deducing total population properties from the evidence available from a sample population.

Informal organization The social groups which develop in an organization and which adopt different norms and behavioural patterns than those advocated by the formal organization.

International trade The exchange of goods and/or services between countries because of comparative advantages on the factors and costs of production.

Inventory control Minimization of stocks, including raw materials/components, work in progress and finished goods, commensurate with the need to ensure uninterrupted production processes, minimal lead time for customers and minimal amount of tied up capital (opportunity costs).

Investment income Money accruing to a company from investments held outside the firm.

Lead time The time period elapsing between the time of placing an order and the receipt of the goods.

Limiting factor A factor which constrains or precludes a particular course of action or prevents attainment of a goal, e.g. machine capacity or availability of finance.

Linear programming An operational research allocation with a view to maximizing (usually) revenue or minimizing costs. The variables have a straight-line relationship.

Macroeconomics The study of the economy as a whole, the inter-relationships of economic aggregates and those factors which affect the total economy.

Margin of safety In break-even analysis, the difference between the firm's current level of activity (output) and the level of activity at which the company would just break even.

Marginal cost The change in total costs which arises as a result of producing one more unit.

Marginal revenue The change in total revenue which occurs as a result of the sale of one more unit.

Market leader The industrial or commercial organization which has the largest share of a particular market for a particular product.

Market orientation The concept of attempting to identify, anticipate and satisfy the needs and wants of actual and potential customers.

Market segmentation Differentiation of the purchasers or users of a product/service in terms of their particular characteristics, e.g. age, SEG, personality, etc.

Marketing mix The interdependent variables, management of which constitutes the total marketing function and which includes the product, its price, promotion, packaging and distribution.

Mean A measure of location or central tendency found by dividing the sum of the frequency of events into the sum of the variables associated with each of those frequencies.

Measures of dispersion Statistical measurements which assess the extent of dispersion of values around a given value, usually the mean, e.g. range, standard deviation.

Measures of location Calculation and identification of a single value from an array of values, e.g. mean, median and mode.

Median When data are arrayed in ascending order of magnitude, the median value is that which occurs in the middle of the data.

Merchant middleman An intermediary in the channel of distribution who takes title to the goods, i.e. buys them, and sells them to the next link in the chain, e.g. a retailer or wholesaler.

Mode That value, in an array of numerate data, which occurs with the greatest frequency.

Monetary policy Macroeconomic policy which concentrates on influencing the level of economic activity by regulating the cost of money (i.e. credit) and availability/supply of money.

Monopoly An economic situation in which one person/firm has total control of a particular product/service. In practice (Monopolies and Mergers Commission) any firm having 25% or more of the supply of a commodity may be investigated.

Monopsony The reverse of monopoly, i.e. a situation where there is only one buyer of a given product/service.

Motivation The act of being induced or the provision of incentives. An individual cannot motivate another person – he can only provide the conditions, or inculcate within another person, the desire or aspiration to do something or achieve an objective.

Needs The physiological and/or psychological requirements which stimulate an individual to behave in a particular way and to achieve goals. Influenced by social and cultural norms.

Net present value is the difference between the present value of revenues and the present value of costs when each has been discounted, at an appropriate rate, from future cash flows to the present time.

Normal curve A frequency distribution in which the number of negative phenomena is the same as the number of positive phenomena. The resulting curve is symmetrical about the mean.

Normal profit The amount of profit which must be generated and paid out in dividends and which is sufficient to maintain the confidence of the shareholders.

Norms The rules and codes of behaviour/conduct which pertain in a particular organization/society. Transgression of the norms will, at the least, earn societal displeasure and at the worst result in extreme sanctions being taken against the offender.

Oligopoly A situation in which a few – usually large – independent organizations control the total market. The concentration of these firms is usually intense.

Open system An organization which interacts freely with its environment and where the passage of information, both in and out, is unimpeded.

Operational research is 'the application of the methods of science to complex problems arising in the direction and management of large systems of men, machines, material and money in industry, business. . .' (UKORS).

Operative A worker at the 'coal face', i.e. on the factory floor/assembly line.

Opportunity costs The costs associated with forgoing an alternative strategy and which should be determined in any investment appraisal (capital budgeting).

Optimize To achieve the best possible under the prevailing circumstances and constraints.

Organization Considered to be a social group which is formed deliberately in order to achieve specific objectives. Having an 'organization' implies that there are accepted procedures and activities through which the objective may be attained.

Overtrading Basically occurs when a business expands more rapidly than the financial situation will allow. As a result, the firm's creditors increase as the amount of money available is tied up in working capital. There is cash flow deficiency and eventually the firm may become insolvent, i.e. unable to pay its debts.

PDM Physical distribution management is concerned with the efficient movement of goods and materials both inwards to the point of manufacture and outwards from the production line to the consumer.

Perception The mental process through which the sensory stimuli are registered and then interpreted by experiential learning and which ultimately precipitates the behavioural responses of an individual.

Perfect market is said to be present where there is a large number of buyers and sellers, when there is perfect information, when the products are homogeneous and there is perfect freedom of entry: such a market does not, however, exist.

Planned obsolescence Corporate plans to phase out or deliberately withdraw a product from the market, usually to prevent misallocation of resources on an ailing product or to launch an up-date version of a similar product.

Point-of-sale The retail outlet at which the product is eventually offered for sale to the final consumer. Value added tax becomes payable at this point.

Pre-test To test out a questionnaire on a very limited population sample before launching the full survey.

Price equilibrium The point at which the level of demand matches exactly the level of supply.

Product extension strategies Methods of extending the acceptability and increasing/maintaining sales of a product by modifying it and/or finding alternative uses/users.

Product life-cycle The concept of the process which a product will undergo over a period of time from development to growth, maturity and finally decline.

Product mix The full range and variety of products which a company offers for sale.

Product orientation The concept of concentrating on the product first rather than the potential market, and then attempting to sell it by aggressive promotion.

Product screening The process by which the suitability of a product is determined after consideration of demand competition, resource variables and corporate policy.

Profit/ volume ratio The relationship between the volume of sales and the level of profit which results when the contribution has met variable and fixed costs.

Promotion consists of the various methods through which an organization seeks to communicate about its products or services in an attempt to maintain or increase sales.

Promotional elasticity The change in the level of demand for a product which occurs as a result of a change in promotional effort and/or expenditure.

Psychogenic Referring to needs considered necessary to satisfy an individual's psychological requirements.

Psychology The positive science which studies the behaviour of people and attempts to understand the mental processes which precipitate that behaviour.

Qualitative In sampling, referring to data which conveys an impression or idea rather than precise information.

Quantitative In sampling, refers to data which is statistically definitive. In management it generally refers to those areas which are mathematical in nature.

Questionnaire A market research tool for gathering information and which is considered by many to be the fundamental and most important constituent of the research.

Random In sampling, where each member of the population has an equal and known chance of being selected.

Revenue The amount of money which an organization receives in return for the provision of a product or service (to be differentiated from income).

Role The part which an individual enacts within a community, i.e. the behaviour which society expects of that individual while occupying a particular position within that society.

Sales forecast An estimate of the probable sales which might be achieved by an organization over a period of time.

Sample A member of a total population, the characteristics of which may be inferred with increasing accuracy by analysis of an increasing number of samples taken under certain conditions.

SEG Socio-economic groups as defined by the National Readership Survey, which segregates the population for marketing purposes according to social status (occupation) and total income.

Self-actualization Described by Maslow as the act of becoming ultimately what one can become, i.e. the pinnacle of self-realization or achievement.

Semi-variable costs Those costs which do change but are not directly proportional to the level of output. They include elements of fixed costs and variable costs, e.g. telephone charges.

Skimming A pricing strategy, usually employed when a firm is able to market a unique product and by which the price is set at a very high level; competition does not, however, allow it to remain high for long.

Skip instructions Instructions contained in a respondent's written questionnaire which direct his attention to the relevant questions only.

Socialization The process through which an individual learns to live with the customs and norms of the society in which he lives.

Sociology The study of those aspects of a society which influence and condition human behaviour within that society.

Socio-technical systems A description of an organization which consists of human and machine components, the correct permutation of which improves overall effectiveness.

Source In communications, the originator or changer in the communication process.

Stable prices A situation where prices are steady and inflation (i.e. a depreciation in the value of money) is minimal.

Status The degree of esteem in a society and the position which an individual is accorded by the members of that society.

Stereotype A generalized and usually irrational classification of an individual, group or organization which is deemed to display certain qualities that are characteristic of it.

Stochastic In sampling, having an element of chance or probability.

Strategic Those decisions/objectives which affect the total organization, usually over or within a long time-scale.

Substitute product A product purchased as a result of a price rise in an original product and which performs a function similar to that of the original.

Supernormal profit Excess of revenue over total costs (including normal profit) which may be utilized at the discretion of the board of directors.

System Consists of a set of interdependent parts which have needs and which will exhibit behavioural patterns. The total system is synonymous with the whole organization.

Tactics Decisions made which affect the firm in the short term and which are more amenable to change than strategic decisions.

Target pricing The setting of a particular price which is to be aimed at in order to produce a satisfactory rate of return.

Turnover The total revenue which a company obtains from its volume of sales.

Utility The usefulness, in terms of satisfaction or fulfilment, of a need which is derived from consuming (possessing) a particular product. As such, it is impossible to define or determine it in quantitative terms other than the value (price) which a consumer is prepared to put on it.

Values The ethical and moral standards which an individual or society espouse and which evolve over a period of time through tradition, education, religion, etc.

Variable costs Those costs which change proportionately with the level of output, particularly wages, raw material costs and energy costs.

Variable pricing The pricing of a product or service on a differential scale in order to entice consumers, increase revenue and ensure that fixed costs are met, e.g. diurnal pricing, off-season hotel rates, mid-week rail travel, variations in telephone charges.